I Can't tell you Anything

ALSO BY THE AUTHOR

"EAST TEXAS: TALES FROM
BEHIND THE PINE CURTAIN"

I Can't tell you Anything

A PENGUIN BOOK BY MICHAEL DOUGAN

MIDTOWN THEATRE

FOXY VIXENS FROM MOTOWN XXX

THIS BOOK IS DEDICATED TO HOMER SPENCE
1941-1991

PENGUIN BOOKS
PUBLISHED BY THE PENGUIN GROUP
PENGUIN BOOKS U S A INC., 375 HUDSON STREET,
NEW YORK, NEW YORK 10014, U.S.A.
PENGUIN BOOKS LTD, 27 WRIGHTS LANE,
LONDON W8 5TZ, ENGLAND
PENGUIN BOOKS AUSTRALIA LTD, RINGWOOD,
VICTORIA, AUSTRALIA
PENGUIN BOOKS CANADA LTD, 10 ALCORN AVENUE,
TORONTO, ONTARIO, CANADA M4V 3B2
PENGUIN BOOKS (N.Z.) LTD 182-190 WAIRAU ROAD,
AUCKLAND 10, NEW ZEALAND

PENGUIN BOOKS LTD, REGISTERED OFFICES:
HARMONDSWORTH, MIDDLESEX, ENGLAND

FIRST PUBLISHED IN PENGUIN BOOKS 1993

10 9 8 7 6 5 4 3 2 1

SOME OF THE STORIES IN THIS BOOK FIRST APPEARED IN THE L.A. WEEKLY,
BALTIMORE CITY PAPER, NEW YORK PRESS, DALLAS OBSERVER,
HOUSTON PRESS, DRAWN & QUARTERLY AND THE ROCKET.

GRATEFUL ACKNOWLEDGMENT IS MADE FOR PERMISSION TO REPRINT EXCERPTS
FROM THE FOLLOWING COPYRIGHTED WORKS:
   "KISSES SWEETER THAN WINE" WORDS BY PAUL CAMPBELL, MUSIC BY JOEL
NEWMAN. TRO - © COPYRIGHT 1951 (RENEWED) AND 1958 (RENEWED) FOLKWAYS
MUSIC PUBLISHERS, INC., NEW YORK, NY   USED BY PERMISSION.

   "TENNESSEE WALTZ" BY REDD STEWART AND PEE WEE KING. COPYRIGHT
1948, RENEWED 1975 BY ACUFF-ROSE MUSIC, INC. (BMI). INTERNATIONAL
COPYRIGHT SECURED. MADE IN THE U.S.A. ALL RIGHTS RESERVED.

EDITOR AND SO FORTH - DAVID H. STANFORD
ASSOCIATE PLOT THICKENERS - JOHN MULLEN, KIT BOSS
PUNCTUATION SWEETHEART- JULIE WROBLEWSKI
BOOK JACKET DESIGN- PAUL "IGUANA BOY" BUCKLEY
LITERARY REPRESENTATION- THE DARHANSOFF-VERRILL AGENCY
LEGAL ADVISORS- MARK MAGHIE, SUSAN GRODE
RIGHTEOUS BROTHER - ROBERT NEWMAN
COVER PHOTO REFERENCE- HUBBARD BENEDICT
LIZARD KING- GREG BURCH
GRAPHIC THERAPY- ART CHANTRY
FIRST BASE - JAMES FOTHERINGHAM, PATRICE DEMOMBYNES
FIREARMS ADVISOR- ROBERT FERRIGNO
POSTER BOY- DENNIS P. EICHHORN
LAST CALL- THE VIRGINIA INN

ISBN 0 14 01.7710 8

PRINTED IN THE UNITED STATES OF AMERICA

MAN IS BORN UNTO TROUBLE, AS THE SPARKS FLY UPWARD.

JOB V. 7.

Contents

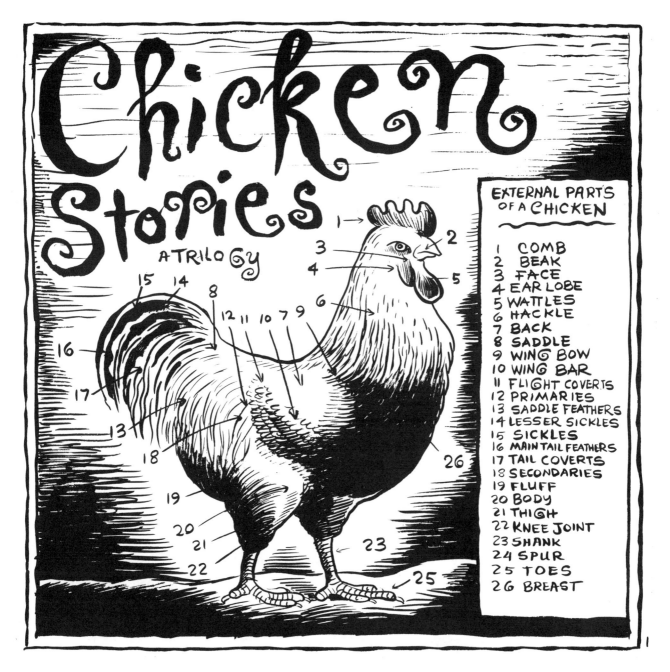

I LOVE CHICKEN. BAKED, ROASTED, GRILLED OR FRIED, IT DOESN'T MATTER.

I ALSO LIKE STORIES. ... ONE NIGHT WHEN I WAS HAVING DINNER WITH SOME FRIENDS, I DISCOVERED THAT WE'D EACH HAD AN UNFORTUNATE EXPERIENCE INVOLVING A CHICKEN.

WHEN I WAS GROWING UP, MY DAD WORKED AS A 4-H AGENT...

TELL IT, BROTHER...

WE LIVED NORTH OF THE HIGHWAY, WHERE THE SUBDIVISIONS AND CAR DEALERSHIPS GAVE WAY TO FARMS...

WE NEVER OWNED A BARN OR A TRACTOR, BUT WE DID RAISE A A FEW ANIMALS - RABBITS AND SHEEP MOSTLY... AND CHICKENS, TOO. UNTIL THE DAY...

STORY: KIT BOSS

The Rooster Got Loose!

3

It was the height of summer. I remember the way the grass - as yellow and stiff as straw - scratched the soles of my feet.

Me and my older brother were racing laps around the outside of the house.

I ran to beat my brother, and partly to beat the boredom that sets in when you can barely remember the first day of summer vacation...

...and can in no way imagine the first day of third grade...

I was chasing my brother ... when all of the sudden ...

4

SOMETHING WAS CHASING **ME**.

THE ROOSTER HAD ESCAPED FROM HIS PEN. HE WAS MAD, HE WAS FREE, AND HE WAS **FAST**...

I TORE THROUGH THE BACK YARD

AAAAAAAAAAUGH!

...UNDER THE CLOTHESLINE...

...AND PAST THE SWING SET.

THEN I GAVE UP...
I FELL DOWN
IN A HEAP...

...KICKING AND PUNCHING TO KEEP THE ROOSTER AWAY FROM MY FACE.

I REMEMBER CRYING OUT FOR MY BROTHER, AND MY BROTHER CRYING OUT FOR MY DAD...

MITCH! HEEELP!

DA-A-A-A-A-ADY!

All at once the pecking and beating of wings stopped. My dad scooped me up and carried me...

...Inside the house, checking me for cuts and scratches.

9

... AND BUTCHERED HIM ON THE STUMP WHERE WE CHOPPED WOOD IN THE WINTER.

THAT NIGHT WE ATE SWEET CORN AND TOMATOES FROM THE GARDEN...

...AND FRESH CHICKEN.

Kentucky Fried Funeral

STORY: MICHAEL DOUGAN

11

12

I MOVED BACK TO TEXAS FROM SEATTLE BECAUSE I'D LEFT HIGH SCHOOL AND COULDN'T FIND A JOB. I THOUGHT WITH A LITTLE FAMILY HELP, I COULD GET WORK IN MY HOMETOWN, SAVE MONEY, AND MOVE BACK TO SEATTLE TO STAY... THE JOB I ENDED UP WITH WAS AT A FUNERAL HOME...

EVERY DAY I'D GO TO WORK AND DO NOTHING ALL MORNING.

THEN ON MY LUNCH BREAK I'D WALK TO THE SUPERMARKET AND HANG OUT IN THE PRODUCE SECTION.

IT WAS RICH WITH THE TEXAS SPRINGTIME HARVEST... WATERMELON, HONEYDEW, GRAPEFRUIT, PEACHES, PLUMS, GRAPES, NECTARINES...

I WOULD FILL MY CART AND GO BACK TO THE FUNERAL HOME TO MAKE A FRUIT SALAD, AND EAT IT IN THE GARAGE.

THE GUYS I WORKED WITH WERE MIDDLE-AGED, CHURCH-GOING, DECENT REGULAR GUYS... THEY WERE NICE, BUT I COULDN'T TALK TO THEM ABOUT MY PROBLEMS... AND MY HOMETOWN FRIENDS WOULDN'T EXACTLY COME TO VISIT ME DURING THE DAY...

THE DEATH BUSINESS DIDN'T BOTHER ME, BUT THE LONELINESS DID.

ON THESE HOT SPRING DAYS I WOULD WAIT FOR THE MAIL TO COME, HOPING FOR A LETTER FROM ALICE, THE GIRL I'D LEFT BEHIND IN SEATTLE. BUT NONE EVER CAME.

I WAS DETERMINED TO WIN HER BACK, BUT IT WAS HARD TO MAKE A CONVINCING CASE FROM A FUNERAL HOME 3000 MILES AWAY. I THOUGHT ABOUT HER CONSTANTLY.

THE ONLY PERSON I COULD TRUST TO KEEP ME INFORMED WAS MARK BALLARD, MY BEST BUDDY IN SEATTLE. I WAS OBSESSED. I GOT INTO A STRANGE HABIT... I WOULD WALK INTO A FURNITURE STORE, OR BAKERY OR CHURCH OR WHATEVER...

MAY I USE YOUR PHONE?

SURE.

THEN I WOULD QUIETLY DIAL *LONG DISTANCE*.

HELLO MARK?

MIKE, WHERE ARE YOU CALLING FROM THIS TIME?

NEVER MIND. HAVE YOU SEEN HER? HAVE YOU TALKED TO HER?

I DID THIS SEVERAL TIMES A WEEK, NEVER CALLING FROM THE SAME PHONE TWICE...

SORRY MIKE, I HAVEN'T SEEN HER.

THANKS!

SURE.

I LATER LEARNED THAT MY RELATIONSHIP PROBLEMS WERE THE FAVORITE DINNER-TABLE TOPIC AT THE BALLARD HOUSE.

WHERE DID MIKE CALL FROM TODAY?

A BAKERY.

HAHAHAHAHAHA

15

AFTER LUNCH I'D SIT IN THE PARLOR WITH THE PORTRAIT OF MY BOSS' GRANDFATHER.

ONE OF THE ODD REQUIREMENTS OF MY JOB WAS THAT I SLEPT IN THE FUNERAL HOME, IN A DORM ROOM, LIKE AN INTERN ON CALL. IT WAS LIKE A HOTEL ROOM, WITH A COLOR T.V., A STEREO, SHOWER, AND A RED EMERGENCY PHONE.

WHAT'S THE RED PHONE FOR?

WE'LL TALK ABOUT THAT LATER...

AT CLOSING TIME I'D LOCK UP AND DIM THE LIGHTS... GO INTO THE BREAK ROOM, MAKE POPCORN AND WATCH THE NEWS.

CLICK

ONE NIGHT I HAD TO INTERRUPT THIS RITUAL TO UNLOCK THE DOOR FOR A GRIEVING FAMILY, WHO'D DRIVEN A LONG WAY TO PAY THEIR LAST RESPECTS...

I GREETED THEM WITH MY STANDARD LOOK OF SOLEMN CONCERN, AND WAITED WHILE EACH VIEWED THE OPEN CASKET...

THEN AN UNMISTAKEABLE SMELL WAFTED INTO THE SLUMBER ROOM...

?

SNIFF
SNIFF

I'D LEFT THE DOOR TO THE BREAK ROOM OPEN, AND THE POPCORN MAKER ON...

I ENDURED SOME HOSTILE LOOKS AS I LET THEM OUT... I LOCKED THE DOOR.

...ONLY TO UNLOCK IT AGAIN FOR ANOTHER LATECOMER...

17

I'D SEEN THIS GUY AT A FUNERAL THE DAY BEFORE. I REMEMBERED HIM BECAUSE HE DROVE A V.W. BEETLE AND CAME ALONE.

IS ROGER HERE?

NO, WE DON'T HAVE A ROGER.

OH. HE USED TO WORK HERE.

HE WAS ODD, BUT I WELCOMED AN AIMLESS CONVERSATION WITH THE STRANGER TO RELIEVE THE BOREDOM. I OFFERED HIM SOME POPCORN...

I'M A FRIEND OF ROGER'S. HE USED TO WORK NIGHTS TOO, HA HA HA...

MY NAME'S TOM.

HI TOM.

HE WENT ON ABOUT THIS GUY "ROGER", AND OTHER EMPLOYEES HE'D KNOWN...

OH YEAH, WE HAD SOME GOOD TIMES...

OH YEAH...

... AND AFTER A WHILE, I REALIZED— I DIDN'T KNOW WHY HE WAS THERE. IT SEEMED HE JUST WANTED TO VISIT.

DO YOU LIKE SEAFOOD? I WAS IN A RESTAURANT IN NEW ORLEANS LAST SUMMER... OR WAS IT BATON ROUGE? ANYWAY, THE OYSTERS WERE MAGNIFICENT DO YOU LIKE OYSTERS?

HE KNEW A LOT ABOUT THE DORMS, AND MENTIONED THAT HE'D "PARTIED" THERE WITH HIS FRIENDS. HE ASKED ME A LOT OF PERSONAL QUESTIONS, AND I WAS BEGINNING TO WISH HE'D LEAVE...

DO YOU HAVE A GIRLFRIEND?

YES...NO. I DON'T KNOW. SHE DOESN'T LIVE HERE...

THAT'S INTERESTING.

THEN THE REASON FOR HIS VISIT BECAME CLEAR.

IF YOU LET ME SLEEP HERE TONIGHT, I CAN MAKE YOU REALLY HAPPY...

HE WAS COMING ON TO ME. HE TOLD ME HE WOULD INTRODUCE ME TO A NEW PLEASURE... HE WANTED TO LICK MY ARMPITS.

I HAD TO ASK HIM TO LEAVE.

WHEN HE WAS GONE, I LOCKED ALL THE DOORS AND WENT TO MY ROOM.

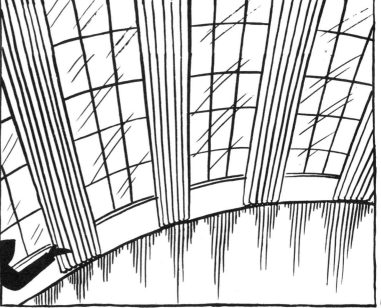

19

*L*ATE THAT NIGHT, THE RED EMERGENCY PHONE RANG.

I'M SENDING ONE OF THE BOYS DOWN TO PICK YOU UP...

IT WAS MY BOSS. THERE HAD BEEN A COLLISION ON THE INTERSTATE...

I PUT ON MY SUIT AND WENT TO THE GARAGE.

HI DON.

HEY MIKE. SORRY TO GET YOU UP.

THE NEXT THING I KNEW, WE WERE AT THE SCENE OF A FATAL ACCIDENT.

*T*HE MOON WAS FULL AND I COULD SEE A CREW DIGGING THROUGH THE BURNED WRECKAGE OF A CAR AND A TRUCK...

*F*INALLY, A PORTION OF BURNED CORPSE EMERGED, AND THE MAN THAT WAS DIGGING TOOK OFF HIS MASK AND THREW UP.

COUGH COUGH

WE ZIPPERED THE REMAINS INTO A BODY BAG, PUT IT INTO THE HEARSE AND STARTED DRIVING BACK INTO TOWN.

UP AHEAD WE SAW HEADLIGHTS COMING IN OUR DIRECTION.

DON PULLED ONTO THE SHOULDER AND TURNED AROUND.

HE TOOK A HANKERCHIEF OUT OF HIS POCKET AND PRESSED IT TO HIS NECK...

WE HAD BEEN GOING THE WRONG WAY ON THE INTERSTATE...

OOPS..

21

THE NEXT MORNING I CALLED MY MOM AND WE TALKED ABOUT GETTING TOGETHER FOR LUNCH. IT WAS A SPECIAL OCCASION AND I WANTED TO DO SOMETHING NICE. ... SHE KEPT ASKING IF I WAS OKAY...

MOM, I'M *FINE*. YES I'M *OKAY*... REALLY...

BUT I WASN'T AND SHE KNEW IT...

CALL IT MOTHERS' INTUITION. INSTEAD OF ME TAKING HER TO LUNCH, SHE TOOK ME TO OUR FAMILY DOCTOR...

HAVE YOU BEEN EATING ALRIGHT?

YEAH, SURE, I GUESS...

HE GAVE ME A VITAMIN B-12 SHOT AND TOLD ME TO EAT REGULAR MEALS.

FRUIT? AND POPCORN?

I'M SORRY! I HAVEN'T BEEN HUNGRY...

THEN SHE TOOK ME TO LUNCH. I HAD A TURKEY SANDWICH AND A GLASS OF MILK.

THEN SHE DROPPED ME OFF AND I WAVED GOODBYE.

HAPPY MOTHER'S DAY.

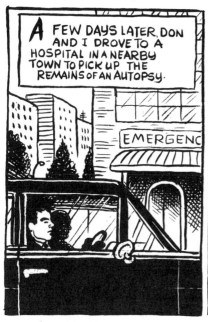

A FEW DAYS LATER, DON AND I DROVE TO A HOSPITAL IN A NEARBY TOWN TO PICK UP THE REMAINS OF AN AUTOPSY.

WE WERE EARLY.

...NOT DONE YET. YOU MIND WAITING A WHILE?

OKAY IF I COME IN?

SURE.

THE FIRST THING I LEARNED, WAS THAT IT'S NOT LIKE SURGERY. IT WAS BLUNT, CRUDE, AND MALODOROUS.

THE ROOM WAS SMALL, AND SEVERAL INTERNS WERE ASSISTING.

MY EYES WANDERED AROUND THE STALE, CLUTTERED ROOM... I SAW A SHELF BULGING WITH MEDICAL SUPPLIES AND CONTAINERS.

ON THE SHELF, WAS A JAR WITH SOME... UNIDENTIFIABLE HUMAN ORGANS SUSPENDED IN FORMALDEHYDE.

IT WAS A MAYONNAISE JAR, WITH MOST OF THE LABEL STILL ON...

23

WHEN THE DOCTOR COMPLETED THE AUTOPSY, I ASKED HIM THE CAUSE OF DEATH. HE PAUSED A MOMENT, AS THOUGH IT HADN'T OCCURED TO HIM.

I DON'T KNOW...

ALTHOUGH I SUSPECT IT WOULD BE RESPIRATORY.

SEE THIS?

HE WAS HOLDING A PIECE OF GREY LUNG TISSUE.

WHAT COLOR IS IT SUPPOSED TO BE?

PINK.

HE SNAPPED OFF HIS GLOVES, STUFFED THEM INTO THE CAVITY, AND WENT TO WASH UP.

WHEN WE DELIVERED THE REMAINS BACK AT THE MORTUARY, THE BOYS WERE SUITED UP AND SMOKING BIG CIGARS.

THE CUSTOMARY CIGAR, I LEARNED, WAS TO FIGHT ONE STRONG SMELL WITH AN EVEN STRONGER ONE.

THEN THEY DISCOVERED THE SURGICAL GLOVES HIDDEN IN THE RIB CAGE ...

WOULD YOU LOOK AT THIS?

NO CLASS AT ALL.

24

LATER THAT EVENING, AFTER I'D LOCKED UP, I GOT A CALL.

IT WAS A WOMAN'S VOICE, ASKING ME IF I WAS AT THE SCENE OF THE ACCIDENT ON THE INTERSTATE...

YES, I WAS THERE. WHO IS THIS?

SHE WOULDN'T TELL ME HER NAME, BUT TOLD ME SHE WAS THE **MISTRESS** OF THE DRIVER OF THE TRUCK.

...HE HAD A **DIAMOND RING** IN HIS POCKET. IT WASN'T RECOVERED... PLEASE HELP ME ...

SHE WANTED **ME** TO HELP HER FIND IT. SHE WANTED IT FOR THE MONEY. I DIDN'T WANT TO GET INVOLVED.

I THOUGHT A LOT ABOUT THE RING... I WONDERED IF IT WAS REALLY OUT THERE.

25

By MID-SUMMER, I'D ALMOST SAVED ENOUGH TO LEAVE, AND I STILL HADN'T HEARD FROM ALICE...I WAS HOT AND MISERABLE, AND HAD TO GET AWAY FROM THE FUNERAL HOME.

PINK COTTON SUMMER SUIT, A GRADUATION GIFT...

I WENT OUT ON MY LUNCH BREAK IN SEARCH OF A PHONE, AND ENDED UP AT **KENTUCKY CHUCK'S CHICKEN** ON MARKET STREET.

MAY I USE YOUR PHONE?

NO PROBLEM.

MARK, IT'S ME. HAVE YOU SEEN ALICE?

HAVE YOU **TALKED** TO HER?

YOU **HAVE**? SHE **WHAT**? WHEN?!

NO...**NO**!

NO, IT CAN'T... SHE CAN'T IT'S... IT'S...

IT WAS THAT DAY THAT I LEARNED IT WAS OVER. SHE'D LEFT ME FOR ANOTHER GUY. I SAT DOWN AND FANTASIZED THAT I'D GONE AND FOUND THE DIAMOND RING AND FLEW TO SEATTLE...I GAVE IT TO ALICE AND SHE CRIED, AND BEGGED ME TO TAKE HER BACK...

BUT NONE OF THIS WOULD BE **TRUE**.

26

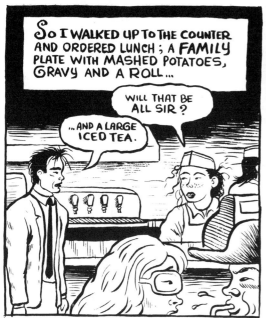

So I walked up to the counter and ordered lunch; a FAMILY plate with mashed potatoes, gravy and a roll...

WILL THAT BE ALL SIR?

...AND A LARGE ICED TEA.

When my chicken arrived, I took one bite and a BURST of HOT, stale grease ran rivers into my sleeves.

K SHAKE OLE SLAW

FRENCH FRIES ONION RINGS —

I looked at the snotty teenager behind the counter and grabbed a handful of paper napkins.

Chuck

I took ANOTHER bite and it was just as bad. The next piece I picked up was even WORSE.

I looked at the greasy flesh and bone and thought I was going to CHOKE.

27

29

The bitter standoff continued while we waited for the cops. I held my ground.

I imagined the **HORRIBLE** things he did to **POULTRY** and the even more **HORRIBLE GROOMING HABITS** that seemed contagious in his **HORRIBLE KITCHEN**...

COUGH COUGH

SCRATCH SCRATCH

SCRATCH SCRATCH

When the officer arrived, I **KNEW** I was defeated.

HEY EDDIE!

HEY CUZ!

SMELLS GOOOD IN HERE...

NOW, WHAT KIND OF SITUATION WE GOT HERE?

THIS **GENTLEMAN** SAYS HE CAN'T EAT OUR CHICKEN AND HE WANTS HIS **MONEY**...

IS THAT RIGHT?

THE HALF-EATEN CHICKEN WAS PRESENTED AS EVIDENCE. I EXPECTED THEM TO PASS THE PLATE AROUND TO THE CUSTOMERS, TOO, AND THEY WOULD BE THE JURY...

SON, YOU CAN'T HAVE YOUR MONEY BACK FOR CHICKEN YOU *CAN'T EAT*, WHEN YOU DONE *ET* MOST OF IT.

THEN THE VERDICT WAS HANDED DOWN.

I WAS HUMILIATED. MY ONLY CHOICE WAS TO SWALLOW MY GREASY PRIDE AND **LEAVE**. SO I DID...

HAHAHA HAHAHAHA HA HA HAHA HAHAHA

HAHAHAHA HAHAHAHA HAHAHA HA HA HA HA HAHA

HA HA HAHA

...HE WAS *RIGHT*. I *HAD* EATEN THE CHICKEN. IT *WAS* HORRIBLE. MY *WHOLE SUMMER* WAS HORRIBLE. I ASKED FOR IT, I PAID FOR IT, AND I ATE IT. NO REFUNDS.

31

HE DIDN'T HAVE ANY TAGS, SO OUR FIRST COUPLE OF DAYS TOGETHER I TRIED GUESSING HIS NAME.

TEDDY?

ROVER?

SCRUFFY?

NONE WORKED.

SPARKY?

BARKER?

SCOOTER?

TINY?

THEN I GOT OUT A PHONE BOOK.

WALTER? DAN? HUEY?
OSCAR? STEVE?
BRADLEY? ALEX?
BOB?

FRANK?
JOHN?
RANDY?

HE FINALLY SORT OF RESPONDED TO FRED. I DIDN'T *LIKE* THE NAME *FRED*, SO I DECIDED TO CALL HIM CHARLIE.

MY CLOSEST NEIGHBOR LIVED A QUARTER MILE AWAY. AFTER A WEEK OF ONLY TALKING TO CHARLIE, I DECIDED TO PAY A VISIT...

AS I WAS ABOUT TO KNOCK ON THE DOOR, I NOTICED THESE BEAUTIFUL CHICKENS AT THE FAR END OF HER YARD...

WELCOME

...AND THE HEN HOUSE ... IT WAS LIKE A MANSION, OR A GIANT DOLLHOUSE...

35

EVEN HER DOOR HAD A BRASS CHICKEN.

KNOCK KNOCK

HI, MY NAME IS JOHN, I JUST MOVED IN UP THE ROAD...

OH MY, I'D INVITE YOU IN, BUT I'M IN THE MIDDLE OF MY SHOW.

WHICH ONE?

RYAN'S HOPE...

OH NO! I WANTED TO SEE TODAY'S EPISODE.

SHE INVITED ME IN. I HAD NEVER SEEN THE SHOW BEFORE, BUT I WAS LONELY AND WANTED TO SEE THE INSIDE OF HER HOUSE. IT SMELLED LIKE BOILED CABBAGE.

MOMENTS LIKE THIS WERE MADE FOR GOLD MASTERCARD

36

HER NAME WAS FLORENCE COLLIER.

I HAVE TO PLAY THE T.V. LOUD OR I CAN'T HEAR WHAT THEY'RE SAYING.

MMHMNMMHMM MMHMMMMMM HMMMMMM

USED EVERY DAY IT ADDS MOISTURE AND KEEPS IT THERE...

SHE HUMMED QUIETLY TO HERSELF DURING THE COMMERCIALS.

I WAS MORE INTERESTED IN HER CERAMICS THAN THE T.V. ...SHE HAD OWLS, ROOSTERS, BLACK KIDS EATING WATERMELON, DISNEYLAND PLATES...

HOME SWEET HOME

...AND A SIGNED PICTURE OF HERSELF WITH WALTER CRONKITE.

Flo, Thanks for the memories xx oo Walter Cronkite

WHERE DID YOU MEET WALTER...

SHHHHHHHH

MY SHOW'S BACK ON...

37

I SAT THROUGH THE REST OF THE SHOW WATCHING VAPOR LINES RISE UP FROM THE RADIATOR.

MY HEAD GOT THAT ACHE I NORMALLY ONLY FEEL IN MALLS AND AIRPORTS, AND THE T.V. STARTED TO SOUND LIKE IT WAS DOWN THE HALL.

HMMMM MMHMM HMMMM

HMMMMHMMM HMMMMM MMMMM

WOULD YOU LIKE SOMETHING TO DRINK?

DISH

THE WATER REVIVED ME.

YOUR HENS HAVE A NICER HOUSE THAN I DO...

38

I SPOIL THOSE GIRLS...

...ONE OF THESE DAYS I'M GOING TO STOP...

*S*HE TOLD ME THEY WERE PRIZEWINNING RHODE ISLAND REDS, AND SHE HAD NAMES FOR ALL OF THEM ···

LET'S SEE... THERE'S MELISSA, KIM...

···AND THERE'S DARLENE, WHO'D MAKE A GOOD LAWYER IF YOU ASK ME...

COOKIES

I BET THEY MAKE GOOD SOUP.

I'VE NEVER KNOWN THEM TO COOK.

*S*HE TOLD ME SHE HAD NEVER EATEN ANY OF HER CHICKENS AND NEVER WOULD.

DO YOU WANT TO MEET THEM?

SURE

...THEY'RE USUALLY HUNGRY THIS TIME OF DAY.

39

I WAS GLAD TO GET OUT OF HER CABBAGE-SMELLING HOUSE.

THEY'LL WARM UP TO YOU QUICKEST IF YOU FEED THEM...

THEN I SAW CHARLIE...

HMMMMM MM HMMM...

...HE HAD GOTTEN INTO THE HEN HOUSE.

OH *GOD!* OH *GAAAWD!*
MY *BAAAABIES!* MY B-B-
B-B-B-B-BUH-BUH-HUH-HUHH

41

42

43

44

45

I TOOK CHARLIE HOME AND THREW HIM IN THE TUB...

ALL NIGHT I TRIED TO THINK OF WAYS TO MAKE IT UP TO MRS. COLLIER FOR WHAT CHARLIE DID TO HER CHICKENS...

47

THE NEXT DAY I WENT TO BURY THE CHICKENS.

THE GROUND WAS ROCKY AND HARD, SO THEY WERE GOING TO BE SHALLOW GRAVES. I HOPED THAT OTHER ANIMALS WEREN'T GOING TO DIG THEM UP AND DRAG THEIR BLOODY CARCASSES AROUND IN FRONT OF THEIR FORMER OWNER.

MRS. COLLIER CAME OUT AND WE MADE A CEMETERY.

ALEXIS

I'VE NEVER HAD ANYTHING LIKE THIS HAPPEN BEFORE. YOU'RE THE WORST NEIGHBOR I'VE EVER HAD.

MAYBE IT'S TIME TO SELL THIS PLACE.

48

49

50

51

HE'S HAVING A *FUNERAL.*

HE DOES THIS FOR EVERYTHING THAT DIES.

...EVEN FISH HEADS HE FINDS IN THE GARBAGE.

THE BOYS HAD MADE AN ALTAR OUT OF AN OLD GATE, CORRUGATED METAL, TIRES, CANDLES, LEAVES AND TWIGS...

I REACHED MY HAND UNDER THE COLD, WET LEAVES...

MY FINGER WENT INTO THE GASH IN DARLENE'S NECK.

53

55

I FINISHED DARLENE'S GRAVE WHILE MRS. COLLIER WATCHED FROM HER WINDOW.

THE NEXT DAY I BOUGHT MRS. COLLIER NEW CHICKENS.

KILLED ALL OF 'EM?

YEAH. I CAN'T KEEP HIM. I'M HAVING HIM PUT TO SLEEP...

NO NO NO NO NO!

I LEFT THE BABY CHICKS AT MRS. COLLIER'S DOOR AND HEADED HOME.

I BET SHE HATES YOU.

SHUT-UP.

I BET SHE WISHES YOU WERE DEAD.

NO, SHE WISHES CHARLIE WAS...

HEY, ANY OF YOU GUYS WANT A DOG?

YOU MEAN FRED?

GRRR...

57

58

I'VE ALWAYS HAD BAD LUCK WITH CARS. IT IS MY HOPE THAT IF I TELL THIS STORY, I CAN BREAK THE SPELL. IT STARTED THE YEAR I TURNED 16... IT WAS THE BEGINNING OF A JOURNEY INTO **MADNESS** AND **DESPAIR**. MAYBE IT'S HAPPENED TO YOU. IF YOU OWN A CAR, IT PROBABLY HAS HAPPENED TO YOU. WELCOME TO THE WORLD OF...

CAR TROUBLE

I BOUGHT MY FIRST CAR IN 1974, WITH MONEY I'D SAVED WORKING AT PIZZA HUT.

WHILE OTHER KIDS WENT TO FOOTBALL GAMES AND PARTIES...

...I WAS SWEATING BEHIND PIZZA OVENS, WORKING FOR THE ONLY 3 MATERIAL THINGS I CARED ABOUT...

... A GIBSON ELECTRIC GUITAR, A FENDER REVERB AMP, AND A RED 1965 CHEVY IMPALA.

YOU WANNA GO TO THE DRIVE-IN?

SURE.

FOR A VERY BRIEF TIME, THE WORLD WAS MINE. THE FIRST THING I DID WAS ASK LESLIE, A WAITRESS AT PIZZA HUT, FOR A DATE...

WE MADE OUT DURING THE MOVIE, THEN WE PARKED IN FRONT OF HER PARENTS HOUSE AND MADE OUT SOME MORE.

THEN I DROVE HOME UNDER THE MIDNIGHT TEXAS SKY WITH NO HEADLIGHTS ON BECAUSE THE MOON WAS SO FULL, I COULD SEE FOR MILES, I COULD SEE FOREVER...

I'D HAD MY RED CHEVY IMPALA FOR LESS THAN A WEEK WHEN I MADE MY FIRST MISTAKE.

EXCUSE ME, DOES ANYONE OWN A BLUE DODGE PICK-UP?

I WAS PULLING OUT OF THE PARKING LOT OF PIZZA HUT, AND I SCRATCHED A CUSTOMER'S TRUCK. I THOUGHT HE WAS GOING TO KILL ME.

I'VE GOT INSURANCE, I'LL TAKE CARE OF IT! SIR? CAN I BUY YOU A PIZZA?

...AT LEAST THE IMPALA WAS O.K.

A FEW DAYS LATER, MOM BORROWED MY CAR TO GO TO THE STORE. SHE CALLED ME FROM A PAY PHONE AT 7-11.

MICHAEL, YOUR CAR IS DOING SOMETHING FUNNY...

WHAT? WHAT'S IT DOING?

IT'S...

WHAT?

WELL...

IT'S ON FIRE.

61

By THE TIME I GOT TO 7-11, THE IMPALA WAS HISTORY.

My TOASTED, MELTED, HORRIBLY DISFIGURED DREAM CAR WAS BEYOND HOPE. MY UNCLE HAD IT TOWED AWAY, I NEVER SAW IT AGAIN... THEN I ENDURED THE NEXT HUMILIATION...

...DRIVING MY MOTHER'S CAR.

IT WAS A CHRYSLER "EXECUTIVE", A HUGE, POWER-EVERYTHING, CRUISE-CONTROL, LUXURY, **MOM** CAR.

SATURDAY MORNING, MARK LUMPKIN AND I DECIDED TO GO FOR A DRIVE. WE WERE ON OUR WAY TO DAIRY QUEEN WHEN WE SAW MY COUSIN BRUCE, WHO HAD ALSO JUST GOTTEN HIS DRIVER'S LICENSE...

HEY, WOULD YOU QUIT SCREWING AROUND WITH THE POWER-WINDOWS? I'VE GOT THE AIR-CONDITIONER ON...

DON'T GET ON **MY** CASE 'CAUSE YOUR **CAR** CAUGHT ON **FIRE!** HA HA HA HA HA...

BZZZZZZ

HONK HONK

HEY! THAT'S BRUCE TUCKER! LET'S FOLLOW HIM...

WE DID A QUICK U-TURN AND FOLLOWED HIM BACK TOWARD THE BRIDGE. THE BIG CHRYSLER TURNED SO HARD, ALL THE COKE BOTTLES IN THE BACK SEAT FLEW TO THE OTHER SIDE OF THE CAR...

AAAAAAAA AAAAAAAA AAAAAAAA AAAAAAAA AAAAAAAA AAAAAAAA

HONK

HONK HONK

THEN WE SAW IT. A HUGE TEXACO TRUCK WAS COMING OUR WAY ON THE NARROW BRIDGE...

IT ALL HAPPENED SO FAST.

WHAT HAPPENED?

YOU NEARLY KILLED US! YOU... LOOK OUT!!!

WHAT?! OH NO...

I'D SWERVED TO AVOID THE ONCOMING TRUCK, BOUNCED OFF THE CURB TO THE OPPOSITE SIDE OF THE BRIDGE, AND SMASHED INTO THE RAIL.

BRUCE TUCKER SAW THE WHOLE THING IN HIS REAR-VIEW MIRROR. IN A PANIC, HE BACKED OVER THE BRIDGE AT FULL SPEED...

63

LOOK OUT!

HE SMASHED INTO MY MOM'S ALREADY TOTALED CHRYSLER.

BUH-HUH-HUH HUUUHUH... MY DAD'S GONNA KILL ME! BUH-HUH-HUHHH...

MY MOM'S CAR!

THAT'S 3 CARS IN ONE WEEK MAN!

MY UNCLE CAME OUT TO INSPECT THE DAMAGE. ...ONE OF THE COKE BOTTLES FROM THE BACK SEAT HAD ROCKETED PAST MARK LUMPKIN'S HEAD DURING IMPACT, AND STRUCK THE WINDSHIELD.

WHAT DID I TELL YOU BOYS ABOUT DRIVIN' AROUND WITH A BUNCH OF EMPTY POP BOTTLES IN THE CAR?!

THAT AFTERNOON, AN OFFICER OF THE LAW CAME OVER TO WRITE ME A TICKET FOR RECKLESS DRIVING, AND A SUIT WAS FILED AGAINST ME FOR DAMAGE TO THE BRIDGE.

I WANT YOU TO READ THIS SON. MAKE SURE YOU UNDERSTAND WHAT IT SAYS, AND SIGN IT.

YES SIR.

64

THE NEXT CAR I OWNED, SEVERAL YEARS LATER, WOULD ALSO BRING ME FACE TO FACE WITH *THE LAW*. IT WAS A 1971 TOYOTA CORROLLA 1200. TO THE CASUAL OBSERVER, IT WAS JUST A CHEAP JAPANESE CAR. TO ME, IT WAS A SPORTSCAR...

WEEEEEEEEEEEEEEEEEEEEEEEEEEEEEEEEEEEEEEEEE

SOON AFTER I GOT THIS TOYOTA, I LEARNED THAT *EVERYTHING* WAS WRONG WITH IT. AFTER SEVERAL MONTHS AND **HUNDREDS** OF DOLLARS IN REPAIR, IT WAS IN RUNNING CONDITION. I TOOK IT OUT FOR A SUNDAY NIGHT TEST DRIVE...

...**ATTRACTING** THE ATTENTION OF **EVERY** POLICE CAR IN THE COUNTY. THE **HIGH-PITCHED** WHINE OF 1200 C.C.'S OPERATING AT **TOP SPEED** COULD BE HEARD FOR **MILES**. IT SOUNDED LIKE A DENTIST'S DRILL OR A **TOY AIRPLANE**... THE COPS SURROUNDED ME LIKE I WAS AN ESCAPED FELON.

IT'S A TOYOTA HAHA HA HA HA HA HA HA HA HA

WHAT DO YOU THINK THIS IS, BOY? A RACE CAR? I'VE GOT A MOTORCYCLE WITH A BIGGER ENGINE THAN THIS.

SORRY, SIR...

YOU WANNA TELL ME WHAT THE HELL YOU WERE DOING?

I TRIED TO EXPLAIN THAT I HAD CHOSEN A SAFE PLACE TO TEST MY CAR, BUT I WAS SO NERVOUS I DON'T KNOW **WHAT** I SAID. I GOT A TICKET FOR GOING 80 IN A 25...

..THE OFFICER'S STATEMENT SAID: "SUBJECT WAS VERY POLITE, BUT WHEN ASKED WHAT HE WAS DOING, HE SAID "THIS IS MY FAVORITE ROAD TO SPEED ON." YOU ACTUALLY SAID THAT?

NOT EXACTLY SIR...

HE TOLD ME I WAS STUPID, FOOLISH, AND RECKLESS, THEN HE FINED ME $350.. I DIDN'T PAY IT. YEARS LATER IT WOULD COME BACK TO HAUNT ME.

65

HAVING SURVIVED THE BONFIRE OF MY BELOVED CHEVY, SMASHING MY MOM'S CHRYSLER INTO A BRIDGE, AND A $350.00 SPEEDING TICKET FOR GOING 80 MILES AN HOUR IN A PUNY TOYOTA.....A SINGLE FOOLISH EPISODE LED ME TO SWEAR OFF CARS FOR ALMOST A DECADE.

HIGH SCHOOL, 1976

MY GIRLFRIEND AND I CUT CLASS AND DROVE HER FATHER'S VAN TO A LOCAL CLINIC TO GET BIRTH CONTROL. BEING THE RESPONSIBLE GUY, I DROVE.

ON OUR WAY BACK FROM THE CLINIC, AN ELDERLY MAN RAN A RED LIGHT.

WE SMASHED INTO HIM, AND THEN WE PULLED OVER, BUT HIS CAR WAS OUT OF CONTROL. HE CRASHED INTO SEVERAL OTHER CARS AND THEN A BUILDING. HIS GAS PEDAL WAS STUCK. SO WAS THE EXPRESSION ON HIS FACE.

I'M SORRY SIR...

HE LOOKED AT ME LIKE I WAS SATAN...

CLEARLY IT WASN'T OUR FAULT, BUT BECAUSE IT WAS HER FATHER'S VAN, WE SWITCHED PLACES TO REPORT THE ACCIDENT. THEY TOOK THE OLD MAN AWAY... I LET MY LICENSE EXPIRE.

I STOPPED DRIVING.

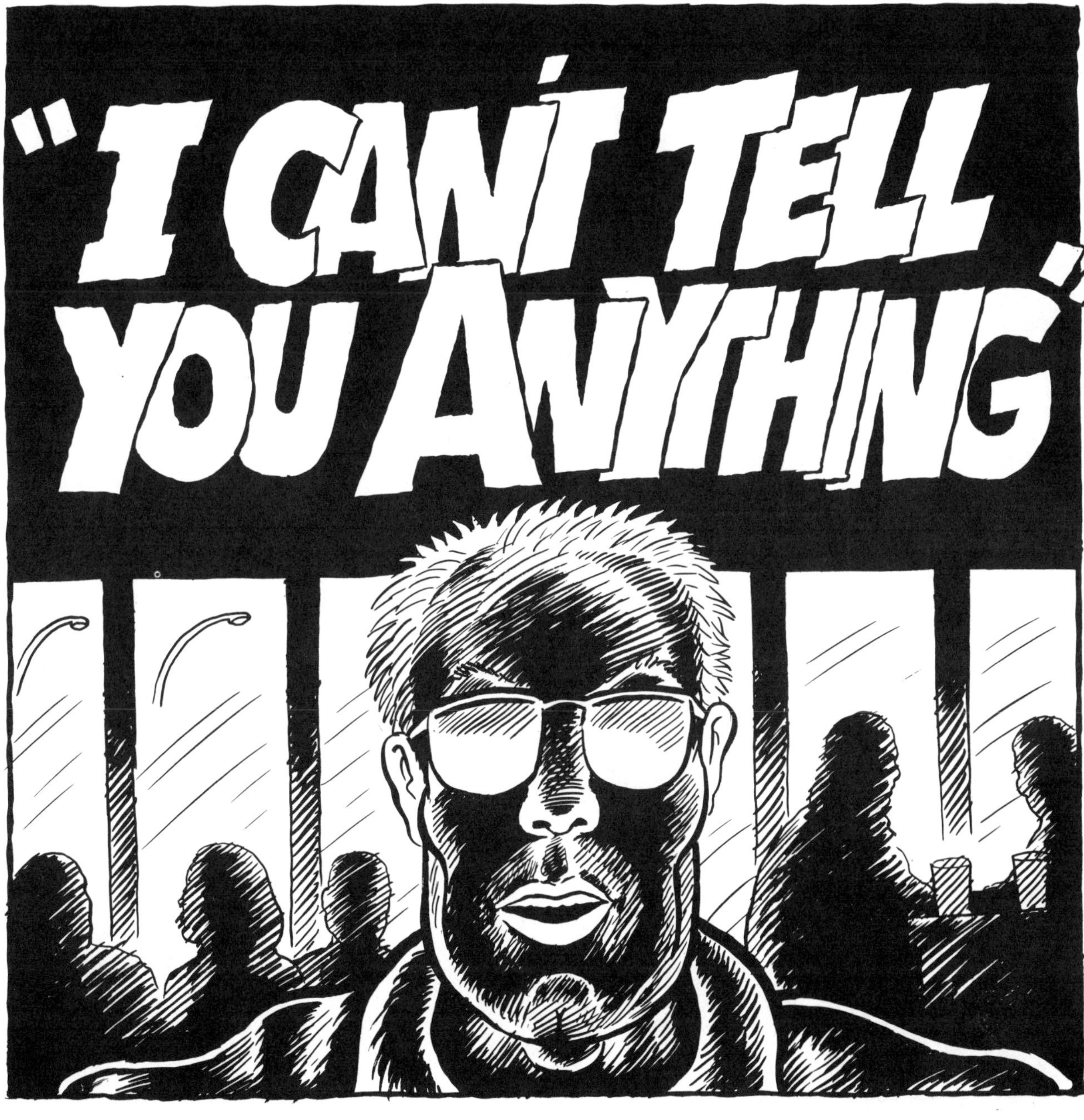
"I CAN'T TELL YOU ANYTHING"

We'd been sitting there for about an hour when he walked in.

It was a warm spring night, the tavern was crowded from a concert that had just let out...

This guy walked in and just stood there with this look of stupified wonderment, an unutterable rapture had **frozen** him in his tracks...

... He looked like he just got out of prison.

I WATCHED HIM LOOK AT THE PEOPLE IN THE BAR, ALL OF THEM YOUNG AND STYLISHLY DRESSED. HE SEEMED OUT OF PLACE.

HE MUST HAVE SEEN ME WATCHING HIM, BECAUSE HE LOOKED DIRECTLY AT ME, AND THEN WALKED TOWARD OUR TABLE.

DO YOU MIND IF I JOIN YOU?

IT WAS HARD TO REFUSE, SINCE WE HAD THE ONLY BOOTH.

HIS SUDDEN PRESENCE MADE US A LITTLE UNCOMFORTABLE, BUT I WAS CURIOUS. THE **FIRST** THING WE NOTICED IS THAT HE WAS **VERY DRUNK**...

WE CONVINCED THE DRUNK STRANGER FROM ALASKA TO SIT DOWN AND PUT HIS MONEY AWAY.

WHAT KIND OF WORK DO YOU DO?

HE PAUSED FOR A MOMENT, AS THOUGH TRYING TO FIGURE SOMETHING OUT...

I'M AN ENGINEER, I... I DESIGN SURVEILLANCE SYSTEMS FOR THE... ...I WORK FOR THE... I'M.. I'M A CONTRACTOR FOR A GOVERNMENT AGENCY, ...I JUST FINISHED A... I... I'VE BEEN UP THERE FOR TEN MONTHS! I JUST GOT INTO TOWN, I WANT A DRINK! I WANT A BOTTLE OF CHAMPAGNE!

71

I WANT TO BUY A ROUND FOR THE HOUSE!

I GOT UP AND WALKED OVER TO THE BARTENDER.

HEY SCOTTY, LISTEN-KEEP AN EYE ON THIS GUY... HE'S FLASHING A **LOT** OF MONEY, AND HE'S ACTING STRANGE.

IS HE OKAY?

I DON'T KNOW.

I LOOKED OVER AND POINTED HIM OUT TO THE BARTENDER ...

HE LOOKED LIKE A CROSS BETWEEN A **LUMBERJACK** AND A **COLLEGE** PROFESSOR. HE **SEEMED** O.K. ...

72

ARE THESE PEOPLE **ARTISTS** OR SOMETHING?

IS THIS AN **ART** BAR?

IT OCCURED TO ME THAT HE MAY HAVE WALKED INTO THE WRONG BAR.

BARTENDER! I WANT TO BUY A ROUND FOR THE HOUSE!

I COULD IMAGINE PLACES IN TOWN WHERE A HARD GUY, FRESH FROM ALASKA WITH **LOTS** OF CASH, WOULD GET A **HERO'S** WELCOME...

AFTER LISTENING TO HIM FOR A WHILE, IT WAS CLEAR THAT HE EITHER WORKED FOR THE C.I.A., OR HE WAS A PATHOLOGICAL LIAR...

73

THE STRANGER SEEMED PUZZLED THAT NO ONE WANTED TO SHARE HIS BOUNTY. HE'D MADE A **LOT** OF MONEY DOING SOMETHING THAT HE WAS TOO DRUNK TO EXPLAIN. I WISHED I COULD HAVE SEEN THIS GUY SOBER BECAUSE **I** WANTED HEAR HIS STORY...

THIS IS PHENOMENAL! IT'S BEAUTIFUL... I HAVENT BEEN IN THE CITY FOR SO LONG. I HOPE I'M NOT INTERRUPTING YOU... I LOVE YOU PEOPLE... I LOVE YOU...

HE RAMBLED ON LIKE THIS FOR A WHILE, THEN FELL SILENT.

DID YOU EVER FEEL LIKE YOU COULD SEE THROUGH SOMEONE ELSE'S EYES? I COULD **FEEL** THE MOMENT WHEN EVERYTHING CAME INTO FOCUS.

I...

76.

HE STOOD AT THE DOOR AND LOOKED BACK. SEEING OUR DISCOMFORT, HE CAME BACK, TOOK THE FIFTY, AND WALKED OUT AGAIN...

HEY, ARE YOU GOING TO BE ALRIGHT? LET ME CALL YOU A TAXI...

NO! I'LL BE FINE, I'M AT THE SHERATON, A FEW BLOCKS FROM HERE.

ARE YOU SURE?

I'M SURE!

ARE YOU GOING TO YOUR HOTEL THEN?

NO.

WHO WAS THAT GUY...

I DON'T KNOW.

I THINK WE SHOULD HAVE KEPT THE FIFTY...

END

LET'S GET LOST

HAVING MANAGED FOR 8 YEARS OR SO WITHOUT A CAR, I DECIDED TO TRY MY LUCK AGAIN. I GOT A DRIVER'S LICENSE. I DIDN'T HAVE A CAR, BUT IT WAS GOOD TO KNOW I COULD BORROW OR RENT ONE IF I NEEDED TO, WHICH I DID, NO PROBLEM.

UNTIL ONE DAY...

THE FATHER OF ONE OF MY OLDEST FRIENDS HAD DIED, AND THE FUNERAL WAS ON THE EAST SIDE. I BORROWED A CAR SO THAT I COULD BE THERE ON TIME. FOLLOWING A HAND-DRAWN MAP, I FOUND THE CHURCH.

WHEN I VIEWED THE OPEN CASKET, IT WAS UNLIKE ANYTHING I HAD EVER SEEN. THERE WAS OLD BILL, SURROUNDED BY HIS FAVORITE THINGS: A GOLF CLUB, A BOTTLE OF GOOD WHISKEY, A CROSSWORD PUZZLE, A PENCIL IN HIS HAND, PHOTOGRAPHS OF HIS LOVED ONES. HE LOOKED HAPPY.

THEN WE DROVE WITH A POLICE ESCORT, HEADLIGHTS ON, TO THE CEMETERY, WHICH TOOK ABOUT 30 MINUTES, EVEN THOUGH ALL TRAFFIC WAS SUSPENDED AND WE NEVER STOPPED FOR A RED LIGHT.

I DIDN'T KNOW WHERE WE WERE.

AMONG THE TREES AND FLOWERS AND TEARS, THEY BURIED OLD BILL. WE WERE DIRECTED TO PROCEED TO THE WIDOW'S HOUSE FOR DINNER, BUT I HAD LEFT MY **HEADLIGHTS ON**. THE BATTERY WAS **DEAD**.

R·R·R·—CLICK.
R·R·RRR·RRR
CLICK·CLICK
...

WHEN I FINALLY **DID** GET IT STARTED, I WAS ON MY OWN. ...I WAS LOST.

I TRIED TO FOLLOW STREET NUMBERS TO FIND THE ADDRESS, BUT IT WAS NO GOOD. IN 2 HOURS I WAS DRIVING IN CIRCLES, YELLING AND SCREAMING, HOLLERING AND SWEARING, ALL THE RAGE AND GRIEF CAME OUT IN BUCKETS, FRIGHTENING LITTLE DOGS AND CHILDREN. I LOST MY MIND.

BY THE TIME I GOT HOME, I WAS CALM. I'D LOST MY VOICE. THE WORST WAS OVER. OLD BILL WAS DEAD.

THE PROBLEM? CARS. THE COLLECTIVE SOUL OF ALL AUTOMOBILES, FOREIGN AND DOMESTIC, HAD CONSPIRED TO RUIN MY LIFE. I HAD TO OUTSMART THEM.

I LIVED DOWNTOWN, WHERE A CAR IS MORE TROUBLE THAN IT'S WORTH ANYWAY. I BRAGGED ABOUT HOW MUCH MONEY I SAVED ON MAINTENANCE, AND TOOK PRIDE IN NOT CONTRIBUTING TO TRAFFIC AND POLLUTION...

IT WAS EASIER THAN ADMITTING I WAS INCOMPETENT BEHIND THE WHEEL, AND HAD A DARK VOODOO CLOUD FOLLOWING ME FROM CAR TO CAR.

I DECIDED TO COMPROMISE. I BEGAN TO SCOUT AROUND FOR A SMALL MOTORCYCLE.

WE'VE GOT A USED BIKE THAT YOU CAN HAVE. ...AN '81 HONDA PASSPORT.

REALLY?

WE DON'T USE IT ANYMORE...

AFTER A FEW MINOR REPAIRS, THE BIKE WAS MINE—WITH A FEW CONDITIONS...

YOU GOT TO TAKE GOOD CARE OF IT...

OKAY...

...DON'T SELL IT. LET US KNOW, WE MIGHT WANT IT BACK.

...NO PROBLEM

IT'S A DEAL.

I WAS ONCE AGAIN FILLED WITH HOPE. HOW COULD I HAVE CAR TROUBLE WHEN I'M NOT DRIVING A CAR?

BARK! BARK! BARK! BARK! BARK! BARK! BARK! BARK!

81

YEARS OF BAD LUCK FINALLY CAUGHT UP WITH ME. JUST AFTER MIDNIGHT ON A SUMMER NIGHT, I GOT BUSTED. A PAIR OF COPS SPOTTED ME WITH EXPIRED TABS AND PULLED ME OVER.

DO YOU HAVE REGISTRATION ON THAT BIKE?

NO SIR.

DRIVER'S LICENSE?

UM... NO SIR, I DON'T...

WHAT'S YOUR NAME?

THEY RAN MY NAME THROUGH THE COMPUTER AND FOUND A WARRANT...

THEY ARRESTED ME. THEY HANDCUFFED ME. THEY ASKED ME A LOT OF QUESTIONS.

WHAT'S YOUR OCCUPATION?

I'M A... I'M A... CARTOONIST.

REALLY?

HERE.

DRAW MICKEY MOUSE.

I COULDN'T BELIEVE IT. THERE I WAS, DRAWING **MICKEY MOUSE** IN HOPES THAT IT WOULD KEEP ME OUT OF JAIL. IT DIDN'T.

...YOU DON'T UNDERSTAND! YOU CAN'T PUT ME IN THERE! THOSE GUYS ARE CRIMINALS.

ISN'T THERE ANOTHER ROOM YOU CAN PUT ME IN?

THE NEXT THING I KNEW I WAS IN A HOLDING CELL, NEXT TO GUYS THAT LOOKED LIKE SEAN PENN AND MR. T.

WHAT ARE YOU IN FOR?

AN UNPAID SPEEDING TICKET, FOR GOING 80 IN A 25.

WHAT WERE YOU DRIVING?

TOYOTA COROLLA 1200...

HA HA HA HA HA HA HA HA HAHAHAHA HA HAHAHAHA HAHAHAHA

THE HOLDING CELL HAD A T.V. MOUNTED TO THE WALL. IT WAS 4:00 A.M. "DUKES OF HAZZARD" WAS ON...

There is absolutely nothing like a refreshing **night in jail** to give the average citizen a healthy respect for **law** and **order**. The first thing you give up are your **consumer rights**. There is no service with a smile.

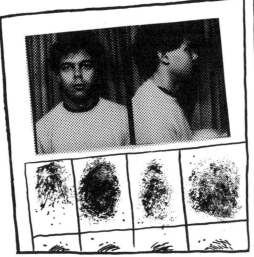

Never had I seen so many bored and **ugly** bureaucrats with guns. They put my belongings in an envelope...

...and issued me an orange pocketless jumpsuit and plastic slippers. Seven hours after my arrest, I was waiting in line to make the phone call.

GUY HAVING WITHDRAWALS

Then I got a thin foam bedroll and a "People" magazine from 3 years ago, and waited...

I had lots of time to think about whether or not to get a tattoo.

Eleven hours later I was out on bail. I walked across town to pick up my impounded scooter, and start my life over again.

83

85

BEFORE I GOT A CHANCE TO ANSWER HE LEAPT OVER THE COUNTER...

EXCUSE ME...

I'M TERRIBLY SORRY...

EEEEEEEEEE!

PLEASE **HELP** ME... YOU'VE **GOT** TO HELP ME!

YOU CAN'T DO THAT! YOU CAN'T HIDE UNDER MY DESK!

I'LL CALL THE POLICE!

YOU REALLY **MUST** HELP ME! ...THOSE MEN ARE TRYING TO **KILL** ME!

PLEASE...

SHOW ME THE WAY OUT OF HERE...

I KNEW AT THAT MOMENT I WOULD DO ANYTHING FOR HIM.

86

DELIVERIES ONLY

THEN HE JUMPED INTO A SPEEDING CAR AND DISAPPEARED...

88

90

91

JOSHUA...I...I... I SHOULD GET BACK TO WORK.

YES. I UNDERSTAND. LET ME DRIVE YOU. I WANT TO DRIVE YOU... CRAZY.

THEN I DID AN IMPOSSIBLE THING...

FASTER!

I PUT MY FOOT DOWN ON HIS GAS PEDAL, COVERED HIS EYES, AND KISSED HIM.

SSCRRRREEEEEEEEEEEEEE EEEEEEEEE

MY GOD DOROTHY, WE COULD HAVE BEEN KILLED!

I KNOW.

CAN I SEE YOU AGAIN?

I...

I'M MARRIED.

I KNOW

MEET ME AT MY HOTEL AT MIDNIGHT.

HE PRESSED A HOTEL KEY INTO MY HAND AND DROVE AWAY.

MIDNIGHT

I WENT BACK TO WORK

I'M SORRY, WHAT DID YOU SAY?

I SAID, WHAT DID YOU HAVE FOR LUNCH TODAY, A TORNADO?

92

93

95

97

98

THAT NIGHT, JOSHUA AND I MADE LOVE FOR THE FIRST TIME...

...BY CANDLE LIGHT ...THIS IS SO ROMANTIC...

OOO OOH DOROTHY OOOOOO BABY!

OH JOSHUA... OOOOOOOOO OOH... OOOOOH...

OH DOROTHY.

OH JOSHUA.

OHOHOWOOOW OOOOOOHOWOHH OH JOOSHHHLAAA

OOOOOOOOO DOROTHY...

OOOH OH! JOSHUA! THE CURTAIN IS ON FIRE!

OH GOD I LOVE IT WHEN YOU TALK DIRTY!

JOSHUA!

99

JOSHUA **NO!**

OH, NOW **THAT** WAS **HEROIC!**

I'M TERRIBLY SORRY...

NOW WHAT ARE WE GONNA DO?

GATHER YOUR THINGS, I'LL MEET YOU IN THE LOBBY.

JOSHUA?

DOROTHY DARLING, YOU'RE AWAKE...

WHERE AM I?

MY HOUSE IN THE COUNTRY.

WHAT COUNTRY?

MEXICO.

MEXICO! HOW DID WE GET HERE?

I DROVE. YOU SLEPT.

EL ESPERANZA GRANDE PLAZA, KILGORE COUNTY'S LARGEST LUXURY HOTEL, BURNED TO THE GROUND YESTERDAY IN WHAT FIREFIGHTERS DESCRIBE AS "THE FLAMES OF HELL LICKING THE STARLIT SKY." THE FIRE STARTED ON THE 2ND FLOOR...

THE CAUSE OF THE FIRE, AUTHORITIES SPECULATE, WAS VIGOROUS LOVEMAKING, WHICH SHOOK THE FURNITURE AND CAUSED A CANDLE TO FALL OVER, SETTING THE CURTAINS ABLAZE. IT WAS FURTHER COMPLICATED BY THE EXPLOSION OF A FIRE EXTINGUISHER, APPARENTLY THROWN INTO THE BLAZE IN A MOMENT OF PANIC...

...HE WAS LAST SEEN CROSSING THE MEXICAN BORDER WITH DOROTHY TREMOR, AN EMPLOYEE OF LITTLE HOPE SAVINGS AND LOAN...

101

103

MEANWHILE, BACK IN LITTLE HOPE...

105

SONNET XXIX

107

JOSHUA THIS IS RIDICULOUS! CAN'T YOU SEE? WE'RE BEING PUNISHED! EVERY TIME WE DO THIS A DISASTER HAPPENS!

NO NO, DOROTHY! IT'S A COINCIDENCE! THESE LITTLE STORMS HAPPEN ALL THE TIME! IT'LL BLOW OVER, TRUST ME!

NO! LET'S GET OUR CLOTHES, FIND YOUR CAR, AND GO HOME! I WANT MY OLD LIFE BACK! I CAN'T DO THIS ANYMORE!

DOROTHY, I BESEECH YOU!

IF OUR LOVE IS NOT MEANT TO BE, MAY LIGHTNING STRIKE ME!

THAT'S IT !!!

I'M GOING HOME! GET ME OUT OF HERE!

NOW!

OH, COME ON DOROTHY, IT MISSED ME BY TEN FEET!

I'M GOING BACK, WITH OR WITHOUT YOU!

108

I PACKED MY THINGS AND WE DROVE, HARDLY SPEAKING TO EACH OTHER, TOWARD LITTLE HOPE.

WE'D STOPPED TO GET GAS NEAR THE MEXICAN BORDER, WHEN TWO LARGE MEN APPROACHED US...

EXCUSE US, MR. MADLEY? COULD YOU JOIN US FOR A MOMENT, IN OUR CAR?

HUUUKKKGH!

JOSHUA!

TAKE MY KEYS!

GO AHEAD WITHOUT ME!

JUST WHO IS IT THAT YOU GENTLEMEN WORK FOR?

SENATOR HARTFIELD'S WIFE, REMEMBER HER?

OH NO...

YOU'VE BEEN A VERY NAUGHTY BOY.

ONE OF HER DAUGHTERS IS PREGNANT...

THE OTHER ONE RAN AWAY FROM HOME...

THE TWINS!

THESE IDLE HANDS...

ONE FOR EACH TWIN.

EEEOOOOO... CRACK CRACK CRASH CRACK CRUNCH CRACK CRACK CRACK CRACK CRACK

109

LATER, BACK IN LITTLE HOPE...

LITTLE HOPE INN

I'M LOOKIN' FOR MY HUSBAND.

ANYBODY HERE SEEN JOHNNY?

WE FELT SORRY FOR HIM, SO WE TOOK UP A COLLECTION...

AND SENT HIM TO THE "LOVE ACADEMY."

HOW CAN WE HELP YOU?

The Love ACADEMY

110

111

112

113

114

LATER THAT WEEK...

DOROTHY? WHAT DO YOU WANT ME TO DO WITH THESE FLOWERS?

WHAT?

DOROTHY, IT'S **NOT** YOUR **FAULT**! DON'T BLAME YOURSELF, IT WAS AN ACCIDENT!

I DID IT. I PULLED THE TRIGGER. I KILLED JOHNNY.

DON'T SAY THAT!

IT'S TRUE.

DOROTHY YOU **REALLY** SHOULD RETURN JOSHUA'S CALLS! HE'S WRITTEN YOU A **BOXFULL** OF LETTERS! YOU **KNOW** HE FEELS **TERRIBLE** ABOUT ALL OF THIS...

THAT MAN IS **NOTHING** BUT TROUBLE. I DON'T TRUST HIM. NO WONDER HIS WIFE WENT **CRAZY**!

DOROTHY HE'S MARRIED? WHO **IS** SHE?

I DON'T KNOW BUT I'D LIKE TO **FIND OUT**.

WELL... WHAT ABOUT THESE FLOWERS?

OH **GOD**, JUST THROW THEM OUT.

115

LATER THAT AFTERNOON...

KILGORE COUNTY INSTITUTE FOR THE MENTALLY DISABLED

VISITORS ONLY ENTRANCE

EXCUSE ME, DO YOU HAVE A MRS. **MADLEY**?

ARE YOU SURE?

LET'S SEE... NO, WE DON'T HAVE A PATIENT BY THAT NAME.

WAIT... I KNOW WHO YOU'RE LOOKING FOR...

HOWARD? COULD YOU HELP THIS WOMAN? SHE'S LOOKING FOR ELIZABETH.

CAN I HELP YOU MISS... MRS...

I'M DOCTOR BENDER, ARE YOU A RELATIVE?

TREMOR, DOROTHY TREMOR.

NO, I'M A FRIEND OF THE FAMILY...

FOLLOW ME...

AUTHORIZED PERSONNEL ONLY NO VISITORS BEYOND THIS POINT

ELIZABETH? THERE'S SOMEONE HERE TO SEE YOU.

We talked for a long time... there was a lot I didn't know about Joshua Madley...

HE'S NOT JOSHUA MADLEY! IT'S AN ACT, HE'S AS COMMON AS DIRT. ...I'M BREAKIN' YOUR HEART, HUH BABY?...

OH LORD!!! I'M SUCH A FOOL...

YOU BELIEVED THAT SWEET TONGUE, DIDN'CHA SUGAR...

BUT I... I...

YOU LOVED HIM, YOU REALLY DID, I KNOW...

I DID TOO.

HOW DID IT HAPPEN? HOW DID YOU FALL IN LOVE WITH HIM?

THOSE EYES... HE JUST LOOKED AT ME...

I'VE SEEN HIM PRACTICE THAT LOOK IN FRONT OF A MIRROR.

OH ELIZABETH, I'VE BEEN HAD!

HOW COME YOU'RE WEARING BLACK? DID SOMEBODY DIE?

MY HUSBAND. I ACCIDENTALLY SHOT HIM.

OH SUGAR. I'M SORRY.

WELL, I'VE GOT A FUNERAL TO GO TO. I HAVE TO GO...

LITTLE HOPE 156

DID YOU AND "JOSHUA" MAKE LOVE?

EVERY TIME WE TRIED, SOMETHING AWFUL HAPPENED...

THAT MAN RUINS EVERYTHING HE TOUCHES...

...AND WHEN HE'S DONE WITH IT...

IT'S HAPPY TO BE RUINED!

HAHAHAHAHAHAHAH HAHAHAHAHAHAH HAHAHAHAHAHAHA HAHAHAHAHAHA AAAAAHAAHAHA HAHAHAHAHAH HAHAHAHA HAHAHAH HAHAHAH HAHAHA AHAHH HAHA

HAHAHAHAHA HAHAHAHAHA HAHAHAHAHAHAHA HAHAHAHAHAHAHAHA HAAHAHAHAHAHAHHAA HAHAH HAHA

MRS. TREMOR, YOU HAVE TO LEAVE ...PLEASE GO...

MISS LIT

120

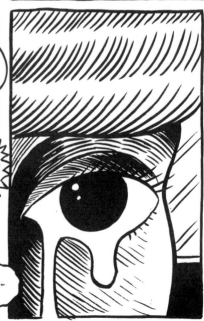

121

122

123

YES I'LL GIVE YOU A PONY! I'LL GIVE YOU THE MOST BEAUTIFUL PONY IN THE WHOLE WORLD!

125

STARTING OVER

So this is what I did. I tried to start all over. My ignorance and negligence had cost me a **night** in **jail**, and I still had fines to pay.

I took a test for my driver's license and went to court to plead for **mercy**. My penalty was reduced and I beat the conviction rap, but I still had little reminders from my night in jail...

WHAT DO I DO?

...BEG LIKE A DOG.

PUBLIC DEFENDER ASSIGNED TO MY CASE

At my birthday party a few weeks later, my friends Maria and Brian gave me a cake with a **file** in it.

Happy Birthday Jailbird! Love Brian xxoo oxxo Maria

Then, I was walking downtown one afternoon and a scruffy-looking character greeted me. I didn't know where I recognized him from, and then I remembered...

HEY MAN.

HEY.

...I knew him from **jail**.

127

EVERYONE TOLD ME TO GET RID OF THE MOTORCYCLE BUT I WOULDN'T LISTEN. I PARKED IT IN THE COURTYARD BEHIND MY APARTMENT AND LEFT IT THERE ALL WINTER.

MEANWHILE I WORKED AND SAVED MONEY TO PAY OFF THE FINES AND PENALTIES I'D RACKED UP.

FINALLY SPRING CAME. I REPLACED THE BATTERY AND **SUCKED** OUT THE OLD GAS AND PUT FRESH GAS IN...

PTOOOOOOO

...IT STARTED **RIGHT UP** AND I WAS ON THE ROAD.

THE DOOM AND VOODOO **HAD** TO BE GONE NOW. I'D **PAID** MY DEBT TO SOCIETY. I WAS **FREE.**

I PUT HUNDREDS OF TROUBLE-FREE MILES ON MY SCOOTER BEFORE BAD LUCK FOUND ME AGAIN.

I WAS WALKING OUT OF A DOWNTOWN APARTMENT BUILDING ONE AFTERNOON, AND WAS ABOUT TO GET ON THE **BIKE** WHEN I NOTICED IT WAS **SMUSHED.** SOMEONE HAD **BACKED** OVER MY SCOOTER...

WEDGED INTO THE SEAT OF MY CRUMPLED BIKE WAS A HAND-SCRAWLED MESSAGE.

I Bumped into your Moped if any damage please call 44...

MOPED?!! ANY DAMAGE? IT'S RUINED!

I WAS LUCKY. THE GUY THAT RAN OVER MY BIKE HAD LEFT A NOTE. AFTER GETTING A DAMAGE ESTIMATE, I HAULED THE WRECKAGE (WHICH I'D NICKNAMED "EXHIBIT A") INTO MY STUDIO, AND CALLED THE NUMBER ON THE CARDBOARD MESSAGE...

HELLO, BOB?

O VER THE NEXT 3 WEEKS I EXERCISED THE TENACIOUS DETERMINATION OF A COLLECTION AGENT, A SKILL I'D LEARNED BY BEING NO STRANGER TO THEIR PERSUASIVE TACTICS MYSELF. (IN **FACT**, I CALLED A COLLECTION AGENT THAT HAD BEEN SQUEEZING **ME** FOR THE LAST YEAR TO ASK FOR ADVICE...) I CALLED BOB AGAIN...

LISTEN BOB, I'M COMING RIGHT OVER

I HAD 3 THINGS WORKING FOR ME. 1. I KNEW WHERE HE LIVED. 2. I KNEW HIS LANDLORD. 3. HE DIDN'T WANT HIS INSURANCE COMPANY TO FIND OUT...

I SUPPOSE YOU WANT A CHECK.

YOU CAN USE MY PEN.

I SUCCESSFULLY COLLECTED ALL THE MONEY FROM HIM, MUCH TO THE SURPRISE OF HIS LANDLORD, WHO LATER TOLD ME HE'D SKIPPED OUT ON HIS RENT... HE DISAPPEARED IN THE MIDDLE OF THE NIGHT.

129

I BOUGHT ANOTHER HONDA PASSPORT, JUST LIKE THE OLD ONE, ONLY THIS ONE WAS RED, HAD NEVER BEEN IN ANY FIGHTS, NEVER BEEN OUT ALL NIGHT, AND DIDN'T HAVE A POLICE RECORD.

NEW RED

OLD YELLER

I FIGURED I WOULD KEEP THE OLD ONE FOR PARTS, BUT I DIDN'T HAVE THE ROOM...

E VENTUALLY I GOT RID OF IT. I GAVE IT TO ERIC, A REPORTER WHO PARKS **HIS** IDENTICAL YELLOW PASSPORT RIGHT DOWN THE STREET. IT MADE PERFECT SENSE.

HEY ERIC

HEY DOUGAN

O UR YELLOW PASSPORTS ARE **SO IDENTICAL,** THAT ONCE WHEN I CALLED THE **SHOP** TO HAVE **MY** BIKE PICKED UP FOR **REPAIR**...

...THEY TOOK **ERIC'S** BIKE BY MISTAKE. HE THOUGHT IT **HAD BEEN STOLEN.**

AAAAAAAAOOOUGH!

WAS PARKED **HERE**

I T TOOK ALL AFTERNOON TO STRAIGHTEN IT OUT.

I THOUGHT YOU WERE PICKING UP MY BIKE!

WE **DID** MR. DOUGAN, AND WE CAN'T FIND ANYTHING **WRONG** WITH IT...

HONDA

THAT'S BECAUSE IT'S **NOT MY BIKE**...

I DROVE THE RED PASSPORT FOR MORE THAN A YEAR WITHOUT ANY TROUBLE. IT WAS ONLY A MATTER OF TIME...

LAST WINTER I HAD MY FIRST MOTORCYCLE ACCIDENT... IT WAS AFTER THE BIG SNOW of '90, THE ROADS WERE FROZEN SOLID FOR A WEEK. WHEN THE ICE FINALLY MELTED, THERE WERE PATCHES OF GRAVEL EVERYWHERE. I LOST CONTROL AND HIT THE PAVEMENT.

THE NEXT DAY I WENT TO A SPORTS DOCTOR. HE PLAYED ME LIKE PRETZEL MEAT FOR A COUPLE WEEKS...

SNAP CRACKLE POP

HE ALSO GAVE ME HIS OPINION ON THE **HEAT** VS. **COLD** DEBATE FOR TREATING INJURIES.

HEAT IS FOR BUTT-BOILS AND STIES IN THE EYE, SON... GET YOURSELF AN ICE PACK.

OKAY

I SHOULD HAVE GOTTEN RID OF THE MOTORCYCLE BUT I DIDN'T. WHEN I RECOVERED, I RODE AGAIN... UNTIL THE FOLLOWING SUMMER, WHEN THE DECISION WAS TAKEN OUT OF MY HANDS...

ARAAAARAUGH!

WAS PARKED HERE

THE MOTORCYCLE WAS STOLEN. I NEVER SAW IT AGAIN.

131

Where the Boys are

I LOVED TO WATCH MY SISTERS GET READY FOR A DATE.

ON A TYPICAL FRIDAY NIGHT, I WOULD BE HANGING AROUND IN THE DOORWAY OF THE BATHROOM, WATCHING MY SISTER TEASE HER HAIR...

...SPRAY IT, AND TEASE IT SOME MORE.

THEN SHE'D TEASE ME.

I'M READY TO GO. HOW DO I LOOK?

133

Susan Beverly transformed herself from jungle woman to beautiful teenage sister in a matter of minutes...

I'M JUST **KIDDING.** I'M NOT REALLY GOING LIKE THIS! WATCH...

... JUST LIKE MAGIC.

My other sister, Donna Jean, had long RED HAIR, and I could **HYPNOTIZE** her just by brushing it.

Then she would sit around with this **DREAMY LOOK** on her face, like my brushing her hair made her go to heaven.

I think she was trying to CON me. It usually WORKED, TOO. She always had that DREAMY LOOK.

My sister Donna Jean was a major league con artist. She could con me into emptying my piggy bank to buy us both some pop...

...Then she'd con me into going to the store to get it

She'd try to trick me into doing her chores...

I'll make a deal with you... I'll clean up the living room if you'll clean up the kitchen, bedroom, dining room and bathroom.

OKAY!

?

WAIT...

...That was her favorite phrase, "I'll make a deal with you."

She also made up interesting swear words.

KITTY CRAP!

THE BOYS THAT DATED MY SISTERS WOULD OFTEN BECOME PALS WITH ME, FOR THIS WAS A SUREFIRE WAY TO EARN VALUABLE POINTS.

...YOU'RE GIVING ME A WATCH?

COOL!

ONE BOY, I THINK HIS NAME WAS RANDY, PLAYED THE GUITAR. HE KNEW ONLY THREE CHORDS, AND HE HAD HIS TONGUE IN THE CORNER OF HIS MOUTH WHILE HE WORKED THEM OUT...

JUST A SEC...

THAT WAS A MAIN FEATURE I REMEMBER ABOUT JOE BOB, HIS TONGUE. HE WAS SUSAN'S BOYFRIEND, AND ANYTIME HE DID ANYTHING HARD, LIKE WORK ON A CAR OR LIFT ANYTHING, THERE WOULD BE HIS TONGUE.

PUT ME DOWN!

QUIT IT! JOE BOB YOU PUT ME DOWN NOW!

DONNA JEAN'S BOYFRIEND, GREG ONCE GAVE ME A PAIR OF BINOCULARS. HE'D JUST GOTTEN OUT OF THE MARINES, AND HE'D USED THEM IN 'NAM. HE ALSO PUT UP A BASKETBALL HOOP BY THE GARAGE.

YEARS LATER, AFTER THEY GOT MARRIED, HE ASKED FOR THEM BACK.

ONE NIGHT I WENT TO SEE MY SISTER PERFORM IN THE DRILL TEAM...

...THEY WERE CALLED THE TOY TIGERS. I WATCHED FROM THE FENCE AS THEY MARCHED IN FORMATION...

I SAW SUSAN. SHE SAW ME. SHE LOOKED RIGHT AT ME.

THEN SHE WAVED AT ME LIKE I WAS HER SECRET BOYFRIEND.

137

I FOUND THAT IF I STOOD RIGHT IN FRONT OF AN AMPLIFIER...

I COULD SCREAM AT THE TOP OF MY LUNGS AND NO ONE COULD HEAR ME.

DID THIS UNTIL I BLEW OUT MY VOCAL CHORDS.

I SCREAMED WITH EVERY BAND AT THE ROCK AND ROLL CARNIVAL UNTIL IT WAS TIME TO GO HOME.

WHEN I WENT TO BED THAT NIGHT, I COULD STILL FEEL THE LOUD GUITARS ECHOING IN MY RIBS...

WHEN I WOKE UP, MY EARS WERE RINGING... IT WAS SATURDAY MORNING AND MY SISTERS WERE SOUND ASLEEP.

139

140

141

We had a piano in the house that mom sometimes played... She knew the songs that were popular during World War II.

"Making Pretend" was my favorite, a truly sad song about a lonely woman waiting for her man to return from the war...

I'm making pretend that you're close to me even though you've been gone a long time I'm making pretend, you'll be here 'till the end ...wish that I had one more rhyme...

It was about this time that I was beginning to make erotic discoveries... When mom was playing the piano, I knew exactly where in the house she was...

...Her hands were occupied and so were mine.

When she stopped playing, so did I...

When she started again, so did I...

Up the Lazy River

WHILE I WAS SORTING OUT MY MOTORCYCLE PROBLEMS, I GOT A CALL FROM A FRIEND WHO WAS DOING SOME ARCHITECTURAL DRAFTING FOR A BAGEL DELI. HE TOLD ME THE OWNER WAS LOOKING FOR SOMEONE TO DO SOME DRAWINGS TO ADVERTISE HIS NEW CAFE. WAS I INTERESTED?

SINCE THE JOB INVOLVED ADVERTISING, AND DRAWING A CUTE DOG, TWO THINGS I GENERALLY AVOID, I CALLED BRIAN, A GUY I KNOW WHO I THOUGHT MIGHT TAKE THE BAIT. HE DID.

I WAS SATISFIED THAT I HAD UNLOADED A TROUBLESOME JOB ONTO A WILLING SUCKER SO THAT I COULD GET ON WITH MY LIFE AND NOT HAVE TO ADVERTISE BAGELS.

3 WEEKS LATER...

IT WAS BRIAN, DRIVING A CHERRY RED 1965 BUICK SKYLARK WITH A WHITE TOP AND CREME INTERIOR...

HEY DOUGAN! CHECK OUT MY CAR!

...REMEMBER THAT BAGEL DELI JOB? THE OWNER TRADED ME 4 DOGGIE DRAWINGS FOR THIS CAR!

IT WAS THE ONE THAT GOT AWAY...

146

I DON'T KNOW HOW I ENDED UP PLAYING POOL WITH JUNE BREWSTER. SHE WAS MY HIGH SCHOOL SWEETHEART, AND I HADN'T SEEN HER IN 15 YEARS.

YOUR TURN

SHE HAD MARRIED, DIVORCED AND REMARRIED THE SAME GUY. HE LOOKED LIKE A COWBOY, BUT WAS ACTUALLY A HOSE SALESMAN FOR AN OIL COMPANY.

IN HIGH SCHOOL SHE TOLD ME SHE WOULD NEVER MARRY. SHE ALSO TOLD ME SHE WAS GOING TO BE A GREAT WRITER, STUDY IN NEW YORK AND LIVE ABROAD.

NOW SHE WORKS AT THE POST OFFICE, AND IS HER LOCAL UNION LEADER.

SHE PUT SOME QUARTERS IN THE JUKEBOX AND ORDERED A BLOODY MARY.

YOU PLAY A PRETTY SERIOUS GAME OF POOL.

MY HUSBAND TAUGHT ME... YEAH, I'M PRETTY GOOD.

HOW COME YOU LEFT THE UNIVERSITY?

I COULDN'T SURVIVE IN WACO. MY ALLERGIES WERE KILLING ME...

BESIDES, I LIKE IT HERE.

I REMEMBERED WHEN SHE MOVED AWAY TO COLLEGE. I WROTE HER EVERY WEEK. SHE HATED BAYLOR AND CRIED ON THE PHONE ALL THE TIME. SHE TOLD ME THAT SHE GOT PREGNANT AND DIDN'T KNOW WHOSE IT WAS.

SHE GOT AN ABORTION A FEW WEEKS BEFORE HOMECOMING. ...I DROVE TO WACO TO SEE HER...

THEN HER HUSBAND ARRIVED AND BEAT ME AT POOL. BEFORE THEY LEFT SHE PASSED ME A NOTE.

Michael
Call me tommorow!

XXXX June
OOO

758-2

147

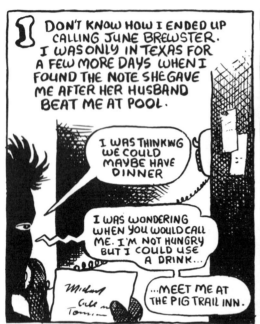

148

I DON'T KNOW HOW I ENDED UP AT THE LIBERTY MOTEL WITH JUNE BREWSTER...

HOW COME YOU GOT MARRIED ANYWAY?

I DUNNO... WHY DOES ANYBODY GET MARRIED.

JUNE... I'M SORRY ABOUT HOW I COULDN'T ...YOU KNOW I... ...I GUESS WE HAD TOO MUCH TO DRINK...

IT HAPPENS TO ME ALL THE TIME

I REMEMBERED THE LAST TIME I HAD SEEN JUNE. I WAS 17, AND IT WAS HER FIRST YEAR OF COLLEGE. WE WERE IN THE PARKING LOT AT HALFTIME OF BAYLOR HOMECOMING... I HAD MY HANDS UNDER HER SWEATER, SMELLING HER HAIR ... WHEN SHE SAID SHE WAS LEAVING SCHOOL AND COMING BACK ...

?

YOU'RE COMING BACK? I THOUGHT YOU HATED IT BACK HOME. WHY ARE YOU DROPPING OUT?

I'LL TELL YOU IF YOU PROMISE NOT TO GET MAD. I'M GETTING MARRIED ...TO RANDY...

YOU'RE GONNA MARRY A HOSE SALESMAN?!

WHERE DID YOU SAY YOUR HUSBAND IS?

LIBERTY MOTEL

AMARILLO... OR FT. WORTH... I DON'T REMEMBER.

THERE WAS A LOT MORE I WANTED TO ASK JUNE, BUT I WASN'T SURE I WANTED TO HEAR THE ANSWERS. BEFORE LONG WE BOTH FELL INTO A DEEP SLEEP...

VACANCY

MOTEL

UNTIL WE WERE AWAKENED BY A NOISE OUTSIDE OUR WINDOW...

WHAT'S THAT

OH GOD... IT'S RANDY'S PICK UP TRUCK...

149

I DON'T KNOW HOW JUNE'S HUSBAND FOUND US AT THE LIBERTY MOTEL. WE HAD BEEN ASLEEP FOR JUST A FEW HOURS WHEN HE CHARGED IN THE DOOR...

RANDY! IT'S NOT WHAT YOU THINK!

OH JESUS THAT'S TELLIN' HIM...

POW!

WAKE UP! WHAT'S THE MATTER?

OH GOD.

WE BETTER BE GETTING BACK...

OH... GOD...

CHEER UP WILL YA?

AS IT TURNED OUT, I MADE IT HOME JUST IN TIME FOR BREAKFAST

WHERE WERE YOU? WE WERE WORRIED SICK...

I HAD A LITTLE CAR TROUBLE. I STAYED IN A MOTEL

YOU SHOULD HAVE CALLED.

ANYWAY, WASH UP, IT'S ALMOST TIME TO EAT...

... LEAD US NOT INTO TEMPTATION, BUT DELIVER US FROM EVIL...

FOR THINE IS THE KINGDOM...

THE POWER...

AND THE GLORY FOREVER...

AMEN.

150

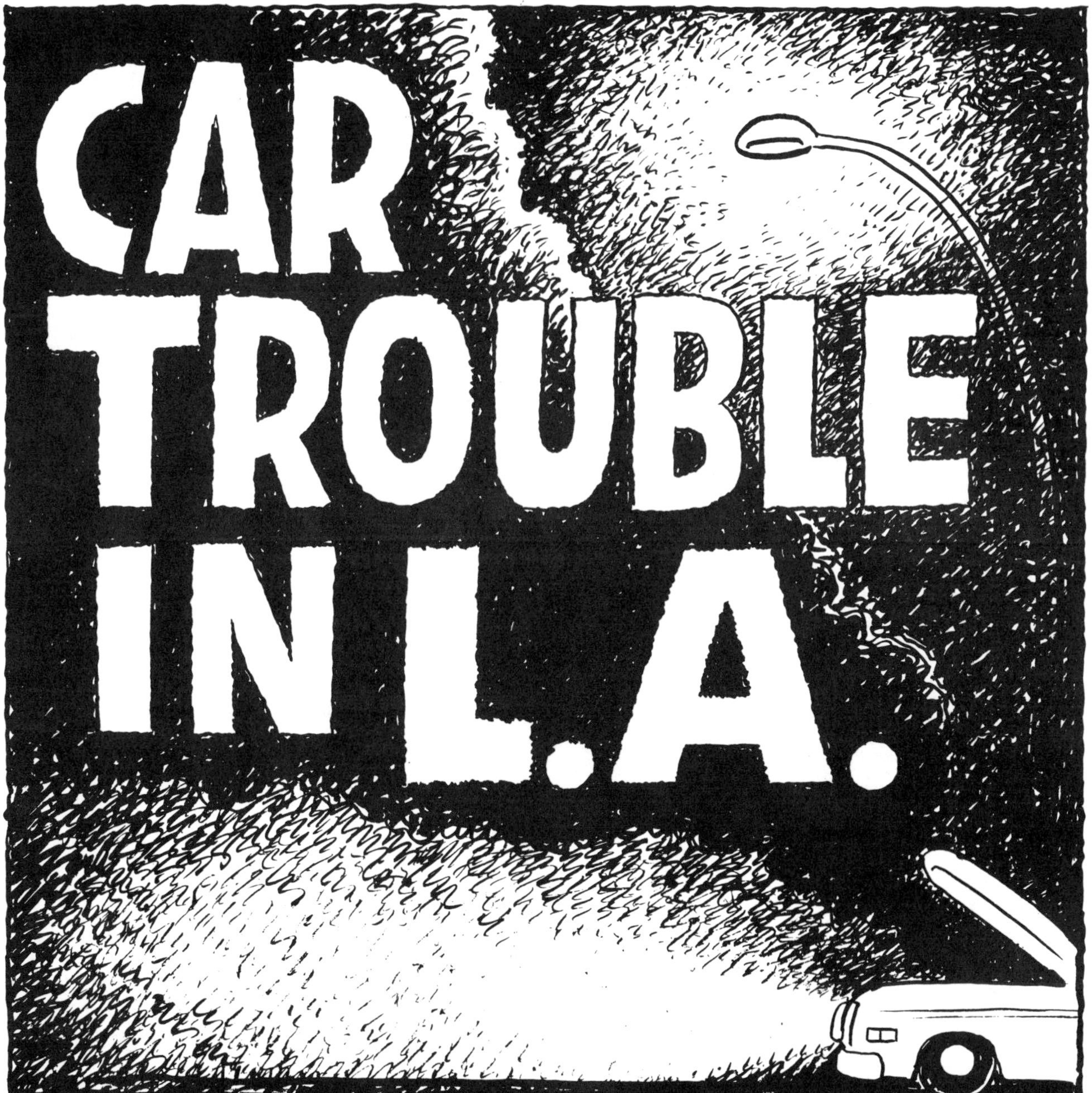
CAR
TROUBLE
IN L.A.

THERE IS NOTHING LIKE THE SMELL OF A NEW RENTAL CAR...ALL OF THE LUXURIES WITH **NONE** OF THE RESPONSIBILITIES! WHAT COULD BE MORE PERFECT?

...IF SOMETHING GOES WRONG, IT'S *NOT YOUR PROBLEM*... BECAUSE IT'S **NOT YOUR CAR**.

VERY OPTIMISTIC

I WAS IN LOS ANGELES TO MEET WITH THE PRODUCERS OF AN ACCLAIMED VARIETY SHOW, TO TALK ABOUT THE POSSIBILITY OF **ME** GETTING **RICH** AND **FAMOUS** WRITING FOR TELEVISION...

I RENTED A FORD ESCORT IN BURBANK, AND WENT ON A DRIVING TOUR OF CENTURY CITY. I WAS HEADING BACK TOWARD GLENDALE WHEN THE CAR BEGAN TO **OVERHEAT**...

GAS
BEER
WINE
CIGARE

I PULLED INTO A SERVICE STATION TO FIGURE OUT WHAT TO DO...

I OPENED THE HOOD, AND A STRANGE MAN IN A BLUE BLAZER WALKED UP TO ME...

My RENTAL CAR OVERHEATS, AND A STRANGE MAN ASKS ME:

WHAT'S THE PROBLEM?

IT OVERHEATED.

HMMM... WE'LL GET YOU ANOTHER ONE...

EXCUSE ME?

I SAID, WE WILL GET YOU ANOTHER ONE.

YOU'LL GET ME ANOTHER WHAT.

WE'LL GET YOU ANOTHER CAR.

YOU'RE GOING TO GIVE ME A CAR?

OUR OFFICE IS RIGHT OVER THERE...

It TURNED OUT, THE GUY WAS FROM THE RENTAL CAR AGENCY. HE RECOGNIZED ONE OF HIS CARS.

WHICH LOCATION DID YOU RENT FROM?

BURBANK

WE'LL GIVE THEM A CALL...

COME ON, I'LL GIVE YOU A RIDE.

THANKS.

It WAS A STRANGE COINCIDENCE, BUT I DIDN'T QUESTION IT. I WAS ABLE TO GET A BIGGER, NEWER RENTAL CAR...

STILL VERY OPTIMISTIC

153

When I finished the meeting at the film studio, I was satisfied that things had gone as well as they could go.

They laughed at my jokes and agreed to pay me money to develop my idea...

I was so pleased that even rush hour traffic didn't get me down... UNTIL my 2nd rental car began to OVERHEAT...

OH NO NO NO NO NNOOO! OH PLEASE GOD NOT AGAIN

AAA AAARAAUGH AAAAAAAAUG

It was the WORST possible time to have a CRISIS on the FREEWAY. I looked frantically for a YELLOW EMERGENCY PHONE...

BAM!! BAM! BAM!

AAAAAAAAA!!

NO LONGER OPTIMISTIC

I was able to find one.

YES THIS IS AN EMERGENCY. AM I WHAT?

ARE YOU OUT OF THE WAY OF TRAFFIC?

YES...

PLEASE HOLD.

WHAT?

THE EMERGENCY PHONE PLAYED MUZAK...

CHERISH IS THE WORD I USE TO DESCRIIIBE

HONK HONK HONK!!

HONK HONK HONK!

HONK!

HOOONK!

There's nothing like the smell of an **overheated** rental car...

I'm listening to an instrumental version of a Simon & Garfunkel song on one of L.A.'s emergency phones, *hours* after my car overheated on the freeway...

Finally, I get an operator...

WHAT IS YOUR LOCATION?

MY WHAT?

ARE YOU SAFELY OUT OF THE WAY OF TRAFFIC?

YES, BUT...

PLEASE STAY WITH THE CAR...

WHERE WAS I GONNA GO?

The rental car people were friendly, but **inept**...

CAN'T YOU JUST CALL A **TOW TRUCK** TO GET ME OUT OF HERE?

...OUR CHICAGO OFFICE HAS TO DO THAT. WHO IS THIS? WHAT IS YOUR LOCATION?

WHAT DO YOU MEAN WHAT IS MY LOCATION?! I'VE BEEN THROUGH THIS 5 TIMES!

WE JUST CHANGED SHIFTS. MY NAME IS MARJORIE, HOW CAN I HELP YOU?

Finally, I convinced them to send a **cab** to take me someplace to wait for one of their tow trucks.

WHERE YOU GOING?

OUT OF HERE...

TAXI

...TAKE ME TO A PAY PHONE, OR A GAS STATION OR SOMETHING...

YOU DON'T WANT TO BE STANDING AROUND A PAY PHONE IN **THIS** NEIGHBORHOOD...

TAXI

I HAVE A SUGGESTION FOR ANYONE IN A CRISIS ON AN L.A. FREEWAY. DO IT RIGHT IN THE MIDDLE OF TRAFFIC. IT WILL SAVE A LOT OF TIME.

155

157

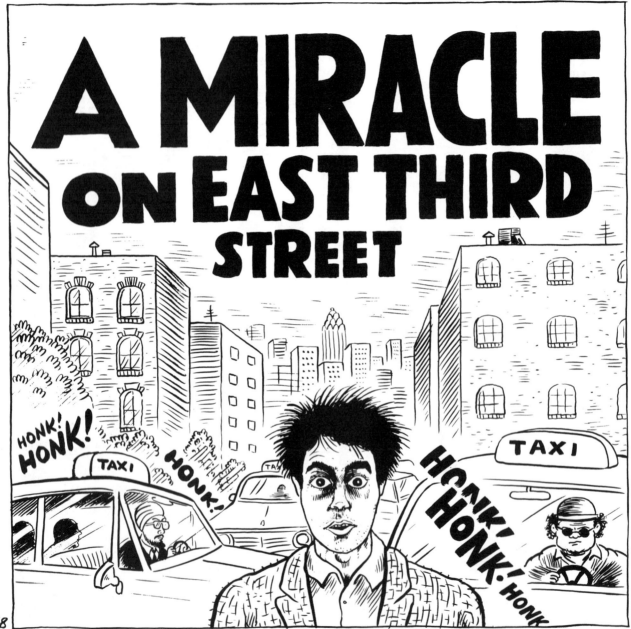

158

MY FIRST VISIT TO **NEW YORK** WAS FOR ONLY 5 DAYS. I STAYED IN A FRIEND'S EAST VILLAGE APARTMENT WHILE HE WAS HOUSESITTING FOR SOMEONE ELSE.

THIS KEY IS FOR THIS LOCK.. NO, THIS ONE IS FOR... WAIT, NO THIS ONE IS...

FIRST MORNING THERE, I GOT UP EARLY TO MAKE APPOINTMENTS WITH PEOPLE I WAS TOLD I **MUST** SEE IF I CAME TO NEW YORK...

I'M SORRY, HE'S NOT IN YET...

...**N**OT REALIZING THAT NO ONE IN NEW YORK IS AT **WORK** AT 8:00 IN THE MORNING. I MADE A POT OF COFFEE AND ENTERTAINED MYSELF WITH THE SUBLIMINAL MESSAGES IN MY HOST'S APARTMENT.

FLOSS!

TAKE VITAMIN

FINALLY I GOT THROUGH TO THE PEOPLE ON MY LIST...

I ALSO MADE A DATE WITH SUSAN, A BALLERINA I HAD KNOWN IN SEATTLE. SHE WAS STUDYING "AMERICAN SOCIAL DANCING" AT COLUMBIA AND LIVED NEAR THE CAMPUS.

159

NINE HOURS LATER...

I'D BEEN TO 3 NEWSPAPERS, 2 MAGAZINES, SEVERAL BOOKSTORES AND RESTAURANTS, ON SUBWAYS AND IN CABS, AND I'D LEFT MY **ADDRESS BOOK** IN ONE OF THEM.

I WAS LOST AND MY FEET HURT, I HAD A SWEATY AND IRRITATING BUTT RASH, I HAD **NO** IDEA WHERE MY ADDRESS BOOK WAS, **NO** IDEA WHICH STREET CORNER SUSAN WAS WAITING AT, AND **NO** WAY TO GET A HOLD OF HER...

WHEN I GOT BACK TO THE APARTMENT, THE MESSAGE LIGHT ON THE ANSWERING MACHINE WAS BLINKING, INDICATING THAT SUSAN HAD CALLED...

SHE HADN'T CALLED. IT WAS ANOTHER FRIEND THAT I'D HOPED TO SEE WHILE I WAS IN TOWN, SO I GAVE UP ON SUSAN AND MADE OTHER PLANS.

OKAY, I'LL SEE YOU IN ABOUT AN HOUR...

FLOSS!

AFTER A SHOWER AND SOME FRESH UNDERWEAR, I HEADED OUT FOR DINNER AND A SHOW, COMPLETELY OBLIVIOUS TO THE FACT THAT SUSAN WAS CALLING ALL OVER SEATTLE...

TAXI

TELLING MY LOVED ONES I WAS INJURED OR DEAD SOMEWHERE IN NEW YORK.

161

LATER THAT NIGHT...

I HAVE GOOSE BUMPS...

YOU LIKED THE PERFORMANCE THAT MUCH?

NO...

THIS THEATRE IS FREEZING.

WE DUCKED INTO A RESTAURANT. I TOLD HER ABOUT MY DATE WITH SUSAN, AND ABOUT LOSING MY ADDRESS BOOK...

...IS IT HOT IN HERE?

DO YOU FEEL OKAY?

I WANTED TO SEE HER PLACE, SO WE TOOK A CAB TO THE UPPER WEST SIDE...

WE WENT OUT ON THE ROOF...

RRRRING

?

MY GIRLFRIEND CALLED ME FROM SEATTLE. SHE TOLD ME THAT SUSAN HAD CALLED HER... SHE ALSO TOLD ME WHERE MY ADDRESS BOOK WAS.

HOW DID **YOU** KNOW WHERE IT IS ?!

HOW DID YOU **FIND** ME?

I CALLED PLACES I THOUGHT YOU MIGHT HAVE GONE. YOU CAN PICK IT UP TOMORROW...

...NOW CALL SUSAN, SHE'S REALLY WORRIED...

BEFORE YOU GO, I JUST WANT TO TELL YOU ONE THING.

WHAT'S THAT?

NO MATTER WHERE YOU ARE ... YOUR GIRLFRIEND CAN ALWAYS FIND YOU.

THANKS.

I CALLED SUSAN FROM A PAY PHONE AT AROUND MIDNIGHT. WE SCREAMED AT EACH OTHER FOR ABOUT 10 MINUTES...

...OUR FRIENDSHIP HASN'T BEEN THE SAME SINCE...

I TOOK A SUBWAY BACK TO THE EAST VILLAGE...

COUGH COUGH!

163

THE THINGS THAT PEOPLE **TELL** YOU TO PREPARE YOU FOR NEW YORK ARE **USELESS**...

"WHEN YOU WALK AROUND AT NIGHT, LOOK ALERT AND **HOSTILE**, KEEP YOUR GUARD UP, THAT'S WHAT EVERYONE DOES..."

I SAW SOME **VERY** VULNERABLE-LOOKING CREATURES WALKING AROUND DISTRACTEDLY, IN BAD NEIGHBORHOODS, AT ALL HOURS OF THE NIGHT.

ANOTHER COMMON MYTH WAS BLOWN EARLIER THAT AFTERNOON...

HAVE A NICE DAY!

COFFEE DONUT

I GOT BACK TO THE APARTMENT AND FELL INTO A DEEP SLEEP.

THE NEXT MORNING...

COUGH COUGH COUGH

AAACHOOO... AAACHOOO

I TOOK A TAXI TO GET MY ADDRESS BOOK.

VILLAGE

HONK HONK

HONK

TAXI

AND SO I GOT IT, THE **ADDRESS BOOK** THAT HAD CAUSED SO MUCH TROUBLE.

Address Book

I TOOK A TAXI BACK TO THE APARTMENT.

TAXI

...EAST THIRD STREET

COUGH COUGH COUGH

YEAH, EVERYBODY'S GOT A COLD...

AS I WAS APPROACHING THE DOOR, I REALIZED THAT SOMETHING WAS WRONG...

165

I HAD LEFT THE **ADDRESS BOOK** IN THE CAB.

I RAN TWO BLOCKS AND TURNED LEFT, I SAW AT LEAST **5 CABS**...

I PICKED ONE, CHASED IT AND **JUMPED ON IT**...

...**IT** WAS THE **RIGHT CAB**.

A SMALL MIRACLE, BUT SOMETIMES YOU HAVE TO TAKE WHAT YOU CAN GET.

167

THE JOINT-OWNERSHIP-OF-A-CHEAP-CAR EXPERIMENT WAS PUT TO THE TEST. JULIE WAS LATE FOR WORK AND **NEEDED** THE IMPALA **DESPERATELY**...

So NATURALLY...

...IT CAUGHT ON FIRE.

WE TOWED THE IMPALA TO A CHEVY DEALERSHIP DOWNTOWN, AND FOUGHT **BITTERLY** IN THE PARTS DEPARTMENT WHILE WAITING FOR THE VERDICT.

AN UGLY TRANSFORMATION OCCURRED... WE DISPLAYED THE KIND OF BEHAVIOR YOU MIGHT SEE ON A BAD DAY AT K-MART.

CHEVROLET PARTS

IT WAS THE LAST TIME WE FOUGHT ABOUT THE IMPALA.

WE HAVE A WHITE TRASH CAR, AND WE'RE HAVING A WHITE TRASH ARGUMENT.

169

DRIVING A REALLY CHEAP CAR AND DRIVING A REALLY EXPENSIVE CAR HAVE ONE THING IN COMMON. **NO ONE WANTS TO MESS WITH YOU.** THE SHEER **UGLINESS** OF THIS IMPALA SENDS THE **UNMISTAKABLE** MESSAGE THAT **I DON'T CARE**...

...AND I **DIDN'T** CARE, UNTIL I **HAD** TO ... AS SOON AS WE REALLY **NEEDED** IT, IT WOULDN'T **START** WE BEGAN TO **FIGHT.** JULIE TOOK THE CAR SERIOUSLY, I SAW IT AS A **JOKE.** WE BEGAN TO DOUBT OUR DECISION TO BUY IT TOGETHER...

I TOOK THE INITIATIVE. I TRIED TO FIX IT MYSELF...

IT WAS THE BATTERY, OR THE ALTERNATOR, OR THE GENERATOR. I GOT A SCREWDRIVER

OKAY, TRY TO START IT NOW...

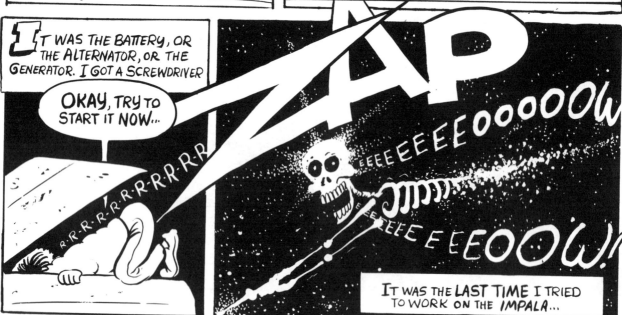

IT WAS THE **LAST TIME** I TRIED TO WORK ON THE **IMPALA**...

171

I WAS DRIVING ALONG MINDING MY OWN BUSINESS WHEN I SAW A LARGE VAN TURNING INTO *MY LANE* INTO *DICKS* PARKING LOT...

I HIT THE BRAKES, BUT IT WAS *TOO LATE* TO STOP. THE GUY IN THE *VAN DIDN'T SEE ME.*

HONK! HONK! HONK! HONK!

CRUNCH CRUNCH HONK!

THE VAN DOOR OPENED...I IMAGINED THE WORST...

INSTEAD, OUT CAME A FRIGHTENED, MIDDLE-AGED WOMAN... SHE WALKED TOWARD ME...

...THEN SHE *HUGGED* ME.

ARE YOU OK?

IT WAS HER FAULT. WE FILLED OUT THE *INSURANCE* REPORTS. A MONTH LATER I GOT A CHECK FOR $387.00 ... IT WAS MORE THAN I PAID FOR THE IMPALA.

172

173

SEVERAL YEARS AGO I HAD TWO JOBS - IN THE MORNINGS I WAS A JANITOR AT A MOVIE HOUSE, CLEANING UP AFTER THE "ROCKY HORROR PICTURE SHOW" AUDIENCE. I LIKED IT BECAUSE NO ONE BOTHERED ME.

MY CLEANING PARTNER WAS RACHEL, A YALE GRADUATE WHO ALSO HAD TWO JOBS.

THEN I WOULD ENDURE MY AFTERNOON SHIFT AT THE ICE CREAM PARLOR. I HATED IT.

HMMM...

FOR MINIMUM WAGE I HAD TO BE NICE TO PEOPLE WHO COULD TAKE FOREVER TRYING TO CHOOSE WHICH FLAVOR THEY WANTED.

I WOULD LOOK AT THEIR GLAZED EXPRESSIONS, SECRETLY THINKING HOMICIDAL THOUGHTS, WHILE THEY MADE UP THEIR MINDS.

OH FOR GOODNESS SAKE, THEY ALL LOOK SO DELICIOUS!

...AND ALL THIS TO THE OPPRESSIVE SOUND OF ELEVATOR JAZZ.

THEN I'D GO HOME, SLEEP, GET UP, CLEAN THE THEATRE, AND GO TO THE ICE CREAM PARLOR AGAIN.

IT SEEMED TO GO ON FOREVER...

THE ONE THING THAT MADE THE JOB INTERESTING WAS THE PARADE OF ECCENTRIC, CRAZY, LONELY, AND DOWNRIGHT MENTALLY ILL PEOPLE THAT FREQUENTED THE SHOP. SOME CAME TO HUSTLE FREE COFFEE, SOME JUST WANTED ATTENTION, SOME SEEMED TO HAVE A ROUTINE IN THE NEIGHBORHOOD THAT RAN LIKE CLOCKWORK, LIKE THE "BLACK CHERRY" MAN...

THE "BLACK CHERRY" MAN CAME INTO THE ICE CREAM PARLOR EVERY DAY. HE WOULD WALK UP TO THE COUNTER, LOOK AT ME WITH EMPTY GREY EYES, AND SAY:

BLACK CHERRY.

HE LOOKED COMPLETELY **GONE**, BUT HERE WAS A MAN WHO KNEW EXACTLY WHAT HE WANTED. HE WANTED A BLACK CHERRY SODA. HE GAVE ME EXACT CHANGE, SAT IN THE SAME CHAIR, AND LOOKED OUT THE SAME WINDOW AT THE SAME TIME EVERY SINGLE DAY...

AMONG THE CRAZY PEOPLE THAT FREQUENTED THE ICE CREAM SHOP WHERE I WORKED: **BARBARA**

THERE Y'GO BARB. DON'T COME BACK TODAY, OKAY? THE BOSS IS HERE.

OK.

COFFEE?

..... WAS A TREMBLING WAIF WHO CARRIED THE SAME STYROFOAM CUP AROUND FOR MONTHS, AND WOULD COME IN EVERY DAY FOR REFILLS...

SUSAN ...A TRULY DERANGED CHARACTER WHO LIVED ON STATE ASSISTANCE, AND WAS THE MOST THEATRICAL MENTAL CASE IN THE NEIGHBORHOOD. SHE COULD LOOK REAL NORMAL, AND THEN—

UNSUSPECTING CUSTOMER

SUE IN ACTION

YOU HAVE SUCH **PRETTY BLUE EYES!**

OH, WHY THANK YOU!

YOU MASTURBATE DON'T YOU!

...MASTURBATION WAS HER FAVORITE THEME. ALTHOUGH I NEVER SAW IT, OTHER RETAILERS TOLD ME SHE WOULD DROP HER PANTS AND MASTURBATE IN PUBLIC ALL THE TIME. SHE CLAIMED TO HAVE KENNEDY'S BABY. NERVE GAS, THE C.I.A., AND HITLER WERE ALSO POPULAR TOPICS...

JACK **STINGMAN** ..... A PAINTER AND ANTIQUE DEALER WHO HAS BEEN IN AND OUT OF INSTITUTIONS SINCE THE 50'S. HE WAS LIKE NIGHT AND DAY. HE SOLD DRAWINGS OUT OF A PAPER BAG, AND TALKED ABOUT RELIGIOUS SUFFERING ONE DAY—AND THE NEXT DAY HE WOULD TRY TO PUT CHAIRS ON THE CEILING OR THROW CHICKEN BONES AT ME, DEPENDING ON HIS MEDICATION. I COLLECTED SOME OF HIS DRAWINGS...

CHRIST WAS KILLED BY NAZIS YOU KNOW. FEMALE NAZIS...

EVERYBODY'S A CRITIC... EVERYBODY'S TALKING ABOUT ME. THEY WANT ME. THEY WANT ME TO SUFFER...

JACK ALSO HAD A FONDNESS FOR WOMEN'S SUNGLASSES.

THEN, LIKE CLOCKWORK, CAME THE **BLACK CHERRY** MAN. I MADE HIS CHERRY SODA, HE PAID WITH EXACT CHANGE, SAT AT **HIS** TABLE, AND STARED OUT THE WINDOW. IT WAS WEIRD...

175

HAVING TWO CRUMMY JOBS DID GET TO ME AFTER A WHILE, AND I WOULD COMPLAIN TO MY CLEANING PARTNER ABOUT IT. WE GOT TO WHERE WE COULD CLEAN THE THEATRE IN A COUPLE OF HOURS, AND THEN WE'D SIT IN THE BALCONY AND SPECULATE ON THE PERSONAL HISTORY OF MR. **BLACK CHERRY**.

YOU MEAN THAT GUY WITH THE TRENCHCOAT AND HAT?

YEAH. HAVE YOU SEEN HIM?

YEAH, HE GOES TO THE CONTINENTAL EVERY DAY FOR LUNCH.

WHAT'S HIS NAME?

I DON'T KNOW...

THEN I'D GO AND DO MY SHIFT AT THE ICE CREAM PARLOR AND THE CRAZY PARADE WOULD START AGAIN. I GUESS I LOOKED FORWARD TO IT BECAUSE THE MAJORITY OF MY CUSTOMERS WERE RUDE, SLOW, AND INDECISIVE.

IT'S NOT LIFE OR DEATH, IT'S ICE CREAM.

HMMM...

NOT EVERY NUTCASE WAS BONAFIDE CRAZY. SOME WERE JUST LONELY. **O**NE WOMAN WHOSE NAME I NEVER KNEW, CAME UP IN A LIMO AND DRANK TWO DOUBLE CAPPUCINOS ON HER WAY TO DANCE CLASS. SHE WAS YOUNG AND VERY BEAUTIFUL, MARRIED TO A WEALTHY MAN MUCH OLDER THAN SHE.

DO YOU LIKE MY HAIRCUT?

HER HUSBAND HAD SOME KIND OF ILLNESS, HE WAS AN INVALID. SHE HAD ALL THIS SEX APPEAL, WITH NO PLACE TO GO, AND SEEMED TO THRIVE ON FLATTERY. SHE'D FLIRT AND BUZZ, DRINKING THESE DOUBLES WHILE HER DRIVER WAITED. THEN SHE'D BE GONE.

THEN THE **BLACK CHERRY** WOULD COME IN - HIS ROUTINE WAS PERFECTLY PREDICTABLE.

BLACK CHERRY.

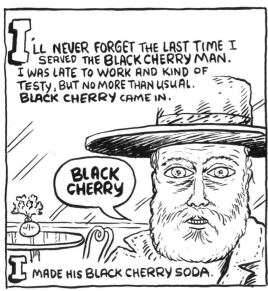

I'LL NEVER FORGET THE LAST TIME I SERVED THE BLACK CHERRY MAN. I WAS LATE TO WORK AND KIND OF TESTY, BUT NO MORE THAN USUAL. BLACK CHERRY CAME IN.

BLACK CHERRY

I MADE HIS BLACK CHERRY SODA.

HE NEVER SAID "A CHERRY SODA PLEASE" OR "I'D LIKE A BLACK CHERRY SODA." IT WAS ALWAYS "BLACK CHERRY." IT BUGGED ME.

YOU SURE ARE PREDICTABLE...

?

EVERY DAY YOU COME IN HERE AND ORDER THE SAME THING.

HE JUST LOOKED OUT THE WINDOW. I TURNED AROUND AND CLEANED THE MILKSHAKE MACHINE, THINKING ABOUT HOW MUCH I HATED MY JOB.

WHEN I TURNED AROUND AGAIN, HE WAS CRYING... HIS MOUTH WAS OPEN, TEARS WERE FLOWING, AND HE WASN'T MAKING A SOUND.

I NEVER SERVED THE BLACK CHERRY AGAIN. HE DIDN'T COME IN, BUT HE WALKED UP TO THE WINDOW EVERY DAY AT EXACTLY THE SAME TIME AND LOOKED AT ME WITH THOSE EMPTY GREY EYES...

I QUIT MY JOB A FEW WEEKS LATER TO START WORKING AT A COFFEE STORE DOWN THE STREET.

177

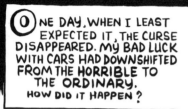

One day, when I least expected it, the curse disappeared. My bad luck with cars had downshifted from the horrible to the ordinary. How did it happen?

Car Trouble: The Final Frontier

My superstition was, if I told this story, I'd break the spell...maybe it's true.

The Impala outlived any expectations I had for it's survival, and continues to run to this day. Julie bought another car and eventually, so did I.

I even got a couple of books on how to buy, maintain, repair, and enjoy automobiles...

— Impala

... BUT I CAN'T HELP THINKING THAT CARS JUST *HAVEN'T LIVED UP* TO THEIR PROMISE. THEY **ALL BREAK DOWN.** IT WASN'T SUPPOSED TO BE LIKE THIS.

HONK HONK HONK

THEY WERE SUPPOSED TO BE PERFECT BY NOW! WHAT HAPPENED TO THOSE **AIR CARS** WE WERE GOING TO HAVE BY THE **1990's** ?!

THE FUTURE IS **HERE** ! I'T DIDN'T **HAPPEN**. WE'VE BEEN **HAD**.

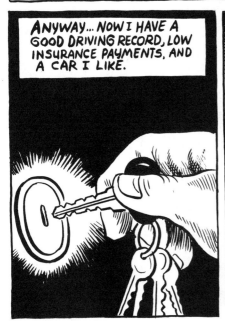

ANYWAY... NOW I HAVE A GOOD *DRIVING RECORD*, LOW INSURANCE PAYMENTS, AND A CAR I LIKE.

I'D RATHER NOT DRAW A PICTURE OF IT, BECAUSE I DON'T WANT TO JINX IT.

I GUESS I'M STILL SUPERSTITIOUS.

I WILL SAY THIS. IT HAD A HALF-EATEN ROLL OF **TUMS** IN THE GLOVE COMPARTMENT WHEN I BOUGHT IT...

I'M KEEPING IT THERE, JUST IN CASE.

179

OPPORTUNITY
Jones
WHO IS THAT GUY?
GUATEMALA
SUMATRA
MOCHA-JAVA
COLUMBIA

In 1983, I was a retail clerk at a coffee store.

Of course I didn't expect to get rich, but I did imagine a better future for myself than shoveling coffee beans.

It was **MORNING in AMERICA** and I was not immune to it's promise, but I was earning barely above minimum wage, with no visible way up...one day a man who could change all that walked into the store...

He was Mr. Opportunity, he was golden, he was a lion, he was my potential mentor, he was **perfect**... **OR**, he was completely full of shit, I didn't know which. When opportunity knocks, what are you gonna do? I had to find out.

181

182

HE PAID FOR HIS POUNDS OF COFFEE WITH A CRISP ONE-HUNDRED DOLLAR BILL, GAVE A RESTRAINED BUT CRIMINAL LOOKING SMILE, AND BREEZED OUT THE DOOR.

...KATIE, OUR ASSISTANT MANAGER, WAS FROM THE SAME PART OF TEXAS AS ME ... SHE HAD A PRETTY GOOD BULLSHIT DETECTOR AND I DIDN'T WANT HER TO KNOW THAT I WAS ACTUALLY IMPRESSED.

WHO IS THAT GUY?

I DUNNO... SOME RICH JERK, PROBABLY...

WE'VE GOT A MANAGERS' MEETING AFTER WORK...

HELP ME UNPACK THIS COFFEE.

RIGHT.

THIS WAS A PERIOD OF RAPID GROWTH IN THE HIGH-END COFFEE TRADE ...

...OUR EMPLOYEE EVALUATIONS ARE TODAY... YOU MIGHT WANT TO FILL OUT YOUR SELF-APPRAISAL FORM...

THE 70's LANGUAGE OF PERSONAL GROWTH HAD BEEN CO-OPTED BY THE 80's BUSINESS SCHOOLS, AND ENDLESS MANDATORY PRODUCT INFORMATION MEETINGS HAD BRAINWASHED US INTO A CAFFEINE-DRIVEN COMPETITIVE FERVOR. WE ACTUALLY BELIEVED THAT SELLING MORE COFFEE HARDWARE WOULD MAKE US BETTER, MORE PROGRESSIVE, MORE EVOLVED HUMAN BEINGS.

LET'S TAKE A MOMENT TO LOOK AT YOUR FILE, SHALL WE, MR. DOUGAN?

OH, ABSOLUTELY.

I WONDER HOW LONG I CAN KEEP THIS STUPID SMILE ON MY FACE

*E*MPLOYEE EVALUATIONS ARE A *BIZARRE,* COMMUNIST-STYLE RITUAL, PROBABLY DEVISED BY *INSECURE, OVERPAID MIDDLE-MANAGEMENT FLUNKIES* TO JUSTIFY THEIR *JOBS.*

TELL ME MICHAEL, HOW DO *YOU FEEL* ABOUT YOUR PERFORMANCE? GROOMING HABITS? YOUR ...ATTITUDE?

WELL, I FEEL THAT I'VE MADE *SIGNIFICANT* PROGRESS. MY SALES FOR EXAMPLE... I'M ... I THINK... IS IT *HOT* IN HERE?

I ENDURED THIS NONSENSE FOR 40 MINUTES, SO I COULD GET A TINY RAISE.

*T*O MAKE MATTERS WORSE, WE WERE GIVEN RAISES THAT WERE ROUGHLY THE SAME, BUT DIFFERED BY AMOUNTS OF 6 OR 7 CENTS. THIS MADE US COMPETE WITH EACH OTHER ... LIKE MY CO-WORKER CORKY, WHO GOT A LITTLE MORE THAN ME ...

MAN! I DON'T GET IT...

IT'S NOTHING PERSONAL I'M SURE. IT'S NO BIG DEAL.

*T*HEN THE COMANY'S MARKETING DIRECTOR, HOWARD HILL, ARRIVED AND MADE AN ANNOUNCEMENT

WE HAVE A *SPECIAL* GUEST TODAY...

PLEASE WELCOME *MOTIVATIONAL SPEAKER* AND *SALES SPECIALIST,* *BOB WALTERS.*

THANK YOU, HAROLD

HOWARD

HOWARD

I BROUGHT BOB IN TO SHOW HIM AROUND...

MY SEMINAR WILL BE AT THE ROASTING PLANT *NEXT THURSDAY.* HOPE TO SEE Y'ALL THERE!

...IN THE MEANTIME, SELL THOSE BEANS! HA HA HA HA HA HA...

That night as I was closing I saw my friend Wes, tapping on the glass...

UH MIKE

We went out for a bowl of soup and I complained about my job.

I JUST WANT AN OPPORTUNITY TO SHOW WHAT I CAN DO!

BUT LATELY, THERE'S AN EMPHASIS ON THE HARD SELL.

UH-HUH...

YOU PEOPLE DO HAVE A LOT OF MEETINGS.

WELL...THANKS FOR LISTENING.

I DON'T KNOW. ...UNTIL I FIND SOMETHING BETTER.

HOW LONG DO YOU EXPECT TO KEEP THIS JOB?

PERHAPS YOU LACK INSPIRATION... THIS WILL ALL PASS ANYWAY...

REMEMBER THIS... THE DOGS BARK...

...AND THE CARAVAN ROLLS ON...

WHAT THE HELL DOES THAT MEAN?

185

186

187

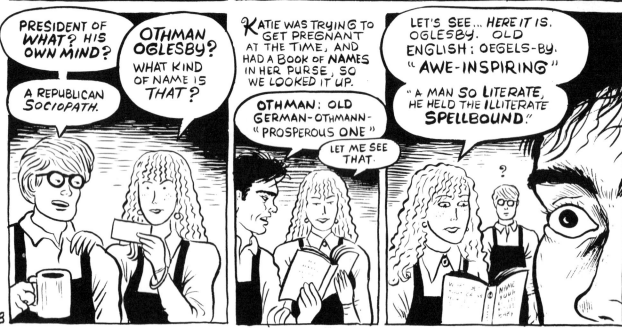

188

189

190

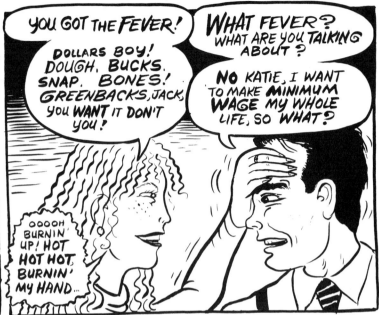

191

192

THE NEXT DAY WE HAD A COFFEE TASTING. AS THE CROPS VARIED FROM SEASON TO SEASON, WE ENRICHED OUR ARSENAL OF ADJECTIVES TO DESCRIBE THE ROASTS OF THE WORLD TO AN INCREASINGLY SOPHISTICATED COFFEE-BUYING PUBLIC.

THIS ONE HAS A DEEP, COMPLEX, BROODING, YET ALMOST FLORAL CHARACTER, WITH A GRASSY, EARTHY, AFTERTASTE.

YES, WITH RICH, MUSKY, ELEGANT UNDERTONES.

SLUUURP SLUURP

SLUUURD SLUURP GULP

CORKY AND I WERE AS COMPETITIVE WITH ADJECTIVES AS WE WERE IN SALES...

WE WERE SUPPOSED TO SLURP AND SPIT, BUT OFTEN WE SLURPED AND SWALLOWED. WE TESTED THE LIMITS OF OUR CAFFEINE TOLERANCE, THEN WE'D ERUPT INTO A FULL-BLOWN VOCABULARY WAR.

ARE YOU KIDDING? FULL-BODIED AND RESONANT? THIS ONE IS MEDIUM-BODIED, NUTTY, AND HAS A FLAT FINISH.

...IT DISAPPEARS INTO A TOTALLY DOWNBEAT AFTERTASTE.

SLUUURP ≈GULP≈

FLAT FINISH! IT DOESN'T EVEN BEGIN TO UNFOLD UNTIL THE FINISH!

THE BEGINNING STAGES ARE FLAT AND UNREMARKABLE, THEN IN THE MIDDLE IT OPENS UP AND BECOMES ROUNDER...

...AND FINALLY RESONATES IN A FULLY-DIMENSIONAL ORCHESTRA OF DEEP BASS NOTES THAT VIBRATE ON THE PALETTE.

MAYBE YOUR PALETTE IS VIBRATING, BUT MY PALETTE FIRED THE BAND AFTER THE FIRST ACT.

SLUUURP ≈GULP≈

193

...THAT'S BECAUSE **YOUR** PALETTE IS **TONE-DEAF** FROM DRINKING THOSE **BRIGHT, NOISY, PERCUSIVE, LATIN-AMERICAN** COFFEES!

WHAT ABOUT YOU? YOUR HIGH-END SPECTRUM WAS **WIPED OUT** IN THE SWIRLING MUDDY **SWAMPWATERS** OF THE **AFRICAN TARPITS!**

YOU WOULDN'T KNOW A **DEEP RESONANT FINISH** IF IT **BIT** YOUR **TONGUE** OFF AND **SHOWED** IT TO YOU!!

BOYS! BOYS! KNOCK IT OFF!

SLURP AND **SPIT!** REMEMBER? DON'T **SWALLOW!** YOU'VE BEEN **SWALLOWING** ALL AFTERNOON.

IT'S NO WONDER YOU'RE SO **HOSTILE**...

...NOW, LET'S CLEAN UP AND PUT THIS STUFF AWAY — WE HAVE TO GO TO THAT **MOTIVATIONAL SEMINAR** IN A FEW MINUTES.

When we went to the roasting plant for the motivational sales seminar, the guest speaker, Bob Walters, was wound up like a toy soldier.

We settled into our folding chairs and awaited his words of wisdom.

Some of us hoped for a performance that would send us into a SALES FRENZY...

PEOPLE... PEOPLE, I WANT YOU TO WELCOME... HOW ABOUT A BIG HAND FOR BOB WALTERS!

THANK YOU HAROLD.

CLAP CLAP CLAP CLAP CLAP CLAP CLAP CLAP LAP CLAP CLAP CLAP CLAP

Some of us wanted only to be ENTERTAINED...

... MOST OF US WANTED TO KILL AN HOUR THAT WE COULD PUT ON OUR TIME CARDS...

HOWARD.

HOWARD.

NONE of us would be DISAPPOINTED.

195

196

197

198

BOB SHATTERED OUR PRECONCEPTIONS ABOUT THE SALESPERSON-CUSTOMER RELATIONSHIP. WE WERE ON THE EDGE OF OUR CHAIRS. THIS GUY WAS **GOOD**.

FOR EXAMPLE—ASSUMING A SALE. WHAT DOES THAT MEAN?

IT MEANS PERCEIVING WHAT A **CUSTOMER WANTS**, AND THEN **SELLING** IT TO THEM, WITHOUT THEIR **KNOWING** IT...

...BUT YOU'RE NOT **JUST SELLING** THEM SOMETHING, YOU'RE **GIVING** THEM SOMETHING. AND DO YOU **KNOW** WHAT THAT **IS**?

PERMISSION! THEY **WANT** IT, YES, BUT THEY **WANT** TO BE TOLD IT'S **O.K.!** THEY WANT **YOUR VALIDATION!**

LET'S SAY YOUR CUSTOMER IS **INTERESTED** IN SOMETHING, BUT THEY'VE **DECIDED,** AT THE **LAST MINUTE,** TO PUT THAT **ONE THING** BACK.

WHAT DO YOU **DO**? YOU **ASSUME** THEY REALLY WANTED IT...

SO YOU **RING IT UP**.

...THEIR TAB REFLECTS THAT UNCONCIOUS DECISION... AND THEN WE HAVE THAT **MAGIC RETAIL MOMENT**...

THEY **REALIZE** YOUR **ASSUMPTION**.

YOU OFFER TO TAKE IT OFF THEIR PURCHASE.

BUT THEY **PAUSE.** THEY HAVE A CHOICE...

...EITHER THEY ASK YOU TO TAKE IT OFF THE FINAL PURCHASE — OR THEY LET IT GO...

IT'S A DELICATE MOMENT. **SAVOR IT...** AND **WHAT HAPPENS?** EXPERIENCE TELLS US — THEY **LET IT GO**.

WHY?

BECAUSE YOU GAVE THEM **PERMISSION!**

THEY REALLY **DID** WANT IT, AND YOU **MADE IT POSSIBLE!**

YOU, THE PERMISSION GIVER, **ALLOWED** THEM TO BUY A **SYMBOL** OF THEIR OWN **POWER** OF CHOICE... WE ALL POSSESS THAT GIFT...

199

...AND THAT BRINGS US TO THE SECRET OF WHAT MAKES US GOOD SALESPEOPLE.

GOOD PEOPLE.

EXCELLENT PROFESSIONALS. THE BEST PEOPLE WE CAN BE.

THIS WAS *IT*. WE WERE READY TO **SELL**. BOB WALTERS HAD OUR **UNDIVIDED ATTENTION**. WE WANTED TO **HEAR THE SECRET**.

I WANT TO TELL YOU ABOUT A SALESMAN... A MAN WHO TAUGHT ME HOW TO BE THE **BEST I CAN BE**...

...A MAN WHO SPOKE OF PERSONAL RICHES SO **RADICAL**, SO **GREAT**, AND **SO TRUE**, THAT HE WAS MISUNDERSTOOD BY THOSE WHO **NEED** HIS MESSAGE THE **MOST**.

HIS IS A STORY OF **TRUTH**, KNOWLEDGE, PROVIDENCE, JUSTICE, AND **GOLDEN, RADIANT FORTUNES**, BEYOND YOUR **WILDEST DREAMS**...

...A MESSAGE OF HOPE THAT CHANGED THE WORLD FOREVER...

...THE MOST SUCCESSFUL SALESMAN THAT EVER WALKED THIS EARTH...

...AND THAT MAN WAS JESUS CHRIST.

THERE WAS A LONG, DEAD SILENCE. NOBODY KNEW WHAT TO SAY. BLINDSIDED BY BOB'S HIDDEN AGENDA, WE WERE CAUGHT BETWEEN BROTHERLY LOVE AND **NAKED COMMERCE**.

WE GAVE MOTIVATIONAL SALES SPECIALIST BOB WALTERS A POLITE SMATTERING OF APPLAUSE AND WENT HOME.

KATIE OFFERED US A RIDE ... ON THE WAY, WE DISCUSSED BOB'S SPEECH.

WHAT WAS THAT HE SAID? "THE ROAD TO INSANITY IS PAVED WITH..."

"...MOTIVATIONAL SPEAKERS TRYING TO SELL RETAIL CLERKS THEIR OWN UNDERWEAR.."

WHAT A PERFORMANCE... HE **MUST** BE A HIT AT SHRINERS CONVENTIONS...

DID YOU **SEE** THE **LOOK** ON HOWARD'S FACE? HE WAS SPEECHLESS!

I COULD HAVE BEEN AT HOME WATCHING **HILL STREET BLUES**...

... AND **WHAT** WAS THAT ABOUT **JESUS** BEING A **SALESMAN?!** WHAT DID HE **SELL?**

DISCOUNT SANDALS?

MYRRH?

"BURNING BUSH-O-MATIC" WEENIE-ROASTERS?

YOU GOTTA HAND IT TO HIM, UP UNTIL THE **SERMON**, IT WAS A PRETTY GOOD SPEECH.

ARE YOU **KIDDING!** HE WAS **WORSE** THAN A **CAR SALESMAN!** HE GAVE ME A HEADACHE...

AFTER WE DROPPED CORKY OFF, KATIE RECONSIDERED HER PREJUDICES ABOUT MY PROSPECTIVE EMPLOYER...

I'M SORRY I'VE BEEN GIVING YOU SUCH A HARD TIME ABOUT THAT **OTHMAN** GUY... IT MIGHT BE A GOOD OPPORTUNITY FOR YOU...

GOOD LUCK WITH YOUR MEETING...HOPE YOU GET A COOL JOB OUT OF IT.

THANKS. I HOPE SO TOO...

201

Monday finally came, and the coffee store was unusually busy... it was near the end of my shift when an odd thing happened.

THANKS FOR COMING IN...

Without planning to, I assumed a sale and it worked just like Bob Walters said it would.

WAIT- I THINK I PAID TOO MUCH...

THIS CAN'T BE RIGHT.

I'M SORRY- MY MIND WAS SOMEWHERE ELSE. I THOUGHT... ...DIDN'T YOU WANT THE MUG?

It was a decorative Italian hand-made thing...

YOU LIKE IT?

OH, THE MUG... LET ME THINK ABOUT IT...

VERY MUCH SO...

OH, WHAT THE HELL. I'LL KEEP IT.

After she left, Corky came over to congratulate me...

YOU BIG SWINGIN' RETAIL STUD! YOU DID IT! YOU GAVE HER PERMISSION TO EXERCISE HER FREEDOM TO BE A SUCKER.

I CAN'T BELIEVE IT.

HEY, WHEN'S YOUR INTERVIEW?

...ABOUT AN HOUR.

I WANT YOU TO HAVE THIS.

WHAT IS IT?

IT'S A TIE TACK... YOU GOTTA GO IN THERE AND KICK BUTT. SHAKE THE COFFEE DUST OFF YOUR PANTS AND GET A WHITE MAN'S JOB, OKAY?

...THANKS CORK.

GOOD LUCK.

IF IT WORKS OUT, MAYBE YOU COULD PUT IN A GOOD WORD FOR ME.

I WILL. THANKS.

202

203

204

LOOK AROUND THIS RESTAURANT, WHAT DO YOU SEE? PEOPLE ENJOYING THE GOOD THINGS IN LIFE? ORDERING ANYTHING ON THE MENU THEY WANT?

OR...

...PEOPLE COUNTING THEIR DOLLARS FOR A SANDWICH AND A CUP OF SOUP, SAVING DIMES FOR BUS FARE AND A NEWSPAPER?

...OR SOME DROOLING GREASEBALL WITH HIS NOSE PRESSED TO THE GLASS, MUMBLING TO HIMSELF ABOUT SOME BULLSHIT INJUSTICE HE CLAIMS TO BE A VICTIM OF...

WE ALL CHOOSE WHAT WE WANT OUT OF LIFE YOU KNOW...

JUST THEN, A PLATE OF COLD OYSTERS ARRIVED...

205

207

209

THE RAW OYSTERS AND CHARDONNAY WERE *SWIMMING* AROUND IN MY STOMACH, AND I WAS BEGINNING TO FEEL LIGHTHEADED...

WHAT DID YOU SAY THE *NAME* OF YOUR BUSINESS WAS?

...BUSINESS, I *HEAR* YOU...

A QUESTION LIKE THAT *DESERVES* AN ANSWER.

OTHMAN HAD OBVIOUSLY GONE TO A LOT OF TROUBLE TO IMPRESS ME, AND I WAS ANXIOUS TO KNOW WHAT THIS WAS ALL ABOUT...

I *KNOW* WHERE YOU'RE COMING FROM! MY *BUSINESS* IS RECRUITING BRIGHT YOUNG MEN LIKE YOU. I'VE *BEEN* THERE.

I STARTED OUT JUST LIKE YOU.

I USED TO THINK I WAS WORTH A *HELLUVA* LOT MORE THAN I WAS BEING PAID. I WANTED TO LIVE IN A NICER HOUSE, DRIVE A BETTER CAR. MICHAEL, I *KNOW* WHAT YOU'RE GOING THROUGH - YOU'RE THINKING, *WHY THEM* AND *NOT YOU!*

210

NO, WHAT I'M *THINKING* IS - *WHAT KIND* OF WORK DO YOU *DO?* EXACTLY *WHAT COMPANY* AM I BEING INTERVIEWED FOR?

OKAY, OKAY... NOW LISTEN CAREFULLY. WHAT WE *ARE,* IS A VERY SPECIALIZED SALES ORGANIZATION. THE KIND OF WORK YOU WOULD BE DOING INVOLVES *SALES,* NETWORKING, AND RECRUITING...

NOW WE WERE GETTING SOMEWHERE

211

213

214

HE OPENED HIS TRUNK. IT WAS FULL OF **AMWAY** PRODUCTS.

WHY DON'T YOU TAKE AN INTRODUCTORY SALES PACKAGE...

NO, NO, I'M NOT INTERESTED!

WAIT— LOOK, WHY DON'T YOU JUST **THINK** ABOUT IT. MAYBE YOU'LL CHANGE YOUR MIND...

SURE... I'LL THINK ABOUT IT AND GET BACK TO YOU.

...**THAT WAS THE END OF MY CAREER** IN **BUSINESS.**

215

MICHAEL DOUGAN GREW UP IN EAST TEXAS, A TERRITORY KNOWN FOR IT'S STORYTELLERS, PREACHERS AND LIARS, AND MOVED TO THE PACIFIC NORTHWEST, KNOWN FOR IT'S GARAGE BANDS, ESPRESSO STANDS AND SERIAL KILLERS. HIS WEEKLY COMIC STRIP APPEARS IN NEWSPAPERS AROUND THE COUNTRY, AND HIS ILLUSTRATIONS HAVE APPEARED IN PUBLICATIONS SUCH AS ENTERTAINMENT WEEKLY, THE VILLAGE VOICE AND THE NEW YORK TIMES. HE LIVES IN SEATTLE.